Education

IN THE DIGITAL AGE

LB

Education

IN THE DIGITAL AGE

DOROTHY WALKER

Sponsored by

BOWERDEAN
Publishing Company Limited

Published by The Bowerdean Publishing Company Ltd.
of 8 Abbotstone Road, London SW15 1QR

First published in 1998

British Library Cataloguing-in-Publication Data.
A catalogue record for this book is available from the British Library.

ISBN 0 906097 89 4

Designed by the Senate
Printed in Malta by Interprint Limited

Work in the Digital Age

A new series of books explaining how the 'new technology' – the Internet, CD-ROM, on-line services, virtual reality etc. – will have an impact on work of different kinds. Titles already published include *Financial Services in the Digital Age* by Paul Gosling, *Retail in the Digital Age* by Nigel Cope, *Travel in the Digital Age* by Linsey McNeil, *Government in the Digital Age* by Paul Gosling and *Publishing in the Digital Age* by Gareth Ward.

CONTENTS

GLOSSARY

CD-ROM: Stands for 'compact disc, read-only memory'. CD-ROM discs look like the CDs played in a stereo system and can hold large amounts of information (multimedia entertainment or edutainment titles, picture libraries or encyclopedias). The data on a CD-ROM, unlike that on a floppy disk, is permanently etched and cannot be altered. See DISK.

DATABASE: Any collection of information, from a phone directory to an exam league table.

DISK: A magnetic platter on which information is written for permanent storage. Portable floppy disks can be used to distribute information to other computer users. The alternative spelling 'disc' tends to be used for CD-ROMs.

EDUTAINMENT: Programs which mix entertainment and education (either 'dumbing down' or 'making accessible' according to viewpoint).

E-MAIL OR ELECTRONIC MAIL: A method of posting messages over a network (usually the Internet). The service is almost instant and very low-cost.

HARDWARE: The physical components of a computer system.

ICT: Information and Communications Technology. In the business world, this is usually abbreviated to IT, as in IT Director or IT Consultant.

INTERNET: A worldwide network of computer networks, available for anyone to use for communicating, and consulting or publishing information. Most popular way of connecting to the Internet is to link a computer to a phone line with a device called a modem.

LAPTOP: A small PC, usually battery-powered, that combines keyboard, screen and system in a single portable unit.

MOUSE: Hand-held, push-button device used to give commands and select items on the computer screen.

MULTIMEDIA: A mix of different media with text, graphics, sound and video animation on one screen. Modern reference software, such as encyclopedias, takes advantage of the multimedia capacity of modern PCs.

ONLINE: Connected to a computer network. A computer user who is online can connect to other, distant computer users, and use 'online' resources, such as courses or reference materials, that are based on distant computers.

PC: Personal computer – a stand-alone machine designed to be used by one person, although it can be linked to others.

SCANNER: A device that transfers photographic images – text, photographs, transparencies – into a computer.

SOFTWARE: Computer programs.

VIDEOCONFERENCING: Face-to-face meeting between two or more people who are in different locations, each sitting in front of a computer with a built-in video camera. Computers need to be linked via high-speed telecommunications lines for videoconferencing.

VIRTUAL REALITY: A computer technology that creates a realistic impression of an artificial world in three dimensions. Largely developed by games manufacturers, virtual reality is increasingly used for real-life applications such as architecture and chemistry.

❶ A Revolution in Learning

FIVE years ago, Maurice King was on the dole. At 55, it looked as though he had no prospects. For most of his life Maurice had worked as an engineer. He began in steelworking, but re-trained as a brewery designer after the steel industry collapsed. When new breweries were no longer needed, he moved again, this time to the construction business, only to find himself made redundant when that industry was hit hard by recession in 1993. When Maurice signed on at his local Job Centre in South Bristol, one in every four adults in the area was unemployed. Today, not only has Maurice found a job, but he has also won a reputation as a trailblazer. His new career spans two of Britain's fastest-growing industries: education and digital information.

Still based in Bristol, Maurice teaches people how to use computers and the Internet. Over the past five years he has tutored everyone from visiting heads of state to home-bound grandmothers, from captains of industry to unemployed teenagers.

▲   ▲   ▲

He works for an organisation called South Bristol Learning Network. Formed in 1993 with government funding, its aim was to teach people about new technology in an area of high unemployment and low morale. Staff were recruited from the local Job Centre, which is where Maurice saw the advertisement. Intriguingly, it called for 'communications skills and an interest in the community', but said nothing about technology. Many of the 50 successful applicants had never been near a computer, but they helped one another to learn. They developed a style of their own, and through down-to-earth workshops they have trained over 6,000 people –including the pensioners that Maurice reaches by taking a computer-equipped van round villages in his spare time. In 1996 the group's winning formula was packaged, and a franchising company called the CyberSkills Association set up to market it to organisations worldwide. Workshops are now being given in towns throughout Britain, as well as in Europe, the USA and Australia. They are run in schools, colleges, community centres and libraries.

But there is more to the success story than that. Maurice tells how many out-of-work teenagers arrive for a course, too nervous even to volunteer their surnames. After a few hours in front of the screen, he says, they leave with a new-found confidence, keen to tell their friends to come along. They have started to equip themselves with the skills they need for their future in the digital age. And the most vital skill has little to do with tapping away at the computer keyboard. As they reflect on the remarkable progress of Maurice and his colleagues – people who began just like them, in the dole queues – the young school-leavers realise that in the future there will be no such thing as 'completing your education'.

LIFELONG LEARNING

In Maurice King's youth, most people set out on their careers with the idea that, having had some kind of education, they would then train for a job, pursue a career with a large company, be promoted if they were any good at it, and then sink into a blissful, well-earned retirement.

Now 38 per cent of the country's workforce works in 'micro companies', which employ fewer than 20 people, and these companies constitute 98 per cent of all firms in Britain. Three million people are self-employed. Many operations are recent start-ups, formed to take advantage of a gap in the market. Increasingly, today's employee has to be a self-starter, a jack of many trades, and prepared in only a few years' time to get to grips with a job that hasn't even been invented yet.

"Media industries in the UK contribute more to the balance of payments than the City," according to Chris Yapp of computer services company ICL. To compete in the new global economy, Britain's workforce will have to be highly-skilled in these new Information and Communications Technologies (ICTs). And to stay competitive, everyone will have to keep on learning throughout their lives to stay ahead of the frantic pace of change.

Exciting new technologies are appearing almost daily. In Germany, it was found that it took seven years to train someone in technology which was changing every three months. But the issue for most educators – and would-be students – is how to get to grips with what is here today, so that everyone benefits. The citizens of the digital age have to learn about technology, but can they also learn with its aid? And what will the consequences be for education?

In the front line of the digital revolution:

❑ **Schoolchildren are learning everything from maths to music by face-to-face teaching, but from teachers who are based hundreds of miles away.**

❑ **With the help of the Internet, teenage pupils are running real businesses with their European counterparts.**

❑ **Whole families are taking Internet courses, written by universities but delivered at local football grounds, shopping centres, libraries and community centres.**

❑ **Old-age pensioners are building and publishing electronic archives of community photographs for use in the education and leisure markets.**

❑ **Students in higher education are attending lectures and tutorials while sitting in their homes and offices.**

❑ Universities, colleges and schools are marketing their expertise to a worldwide audience on the Internet.

❑ Youngsters with profound disabilities are writing to new-found pen pals, finding their own way around, even choreographing musical evenings with the help of technology.

❑ Work has started on exploring how schooling patterns could be changed by having pupils spend some of their time learning independently, perhaps at home, with the aid of computer-based materials.

❑ Libraries and museums are aiming to be major players in the educational software business, by creating digital collections of their treasures.

❑ Home schooling is booming, as families realise the potential of computers and the Internet to bring information and help on to the kitchen tabletop.

❑ Universities are building learning networks for companies, and employees are being paid to take self-paced courses on any topic that interests them, to encourage them to learn how to learn.

Scattered around the country are pockets of expertise, and examples of projects that are proving their worth. Most successful schemes have already been blessed not only with an injection of funds, but also with a good helping of common sense. For the main danger with new technology lies in assuming that in itself, it is somehow 'educational': that the bigger the computer or the better the network, the more learning benefits will automatically accrue.

NATIONAL GRID FOR LEARNING

The focus for Britain's lifelong learners in the digital age will be the National Grid for Learning, a network of computer networks, linked by the Internet. The Grid will deliver materials and services to support teachers and learners in schools, colleges, universities, libraries, the workplace and the home. A prototype was launched in January 1998, and all schools, colleges, universities and libraries are to be connected to the Grid by 2002.

The idea of a national grid was first aired in 1994 by Chris Yapp, lifelong learning consultant at ICL, and his colleague Malcolm Napier, who formerly worked for the Central Electricity Generating Board. Yapp explains the thinking behind the idea: "If you contrast my father's life with mine, you start to see what has happened. People went through primary and secondary school, the army, apprenticeship and work. By the age of 30 they had sufficient skills to be able to learn on the job and pay off a mortgage, raise a family and earn a pension. For people approaching retirement that is the life many have led and the life the legislation and pensions systems encouraged. But it is a fallacy that life was always like that. In 1900, 50 per cent were employed, and 50 per cent were in casual work. Now we are back to that again −50 per cent are in casual, part-time or multiple portfolio careers. People have to re-train themselves more often. If they don't manage that, they end up with lots of enforced leisure or retirement. Those in work are working longer and longer hours, and others not working at all. Those in work are able to get access to education and training, those out of work are not – the gulf widens.

"Britain is a multimedia nation, driven by the English language – 800 million people somewhere on the planet today are learning English for some purpose or other. We are a major player in all media – publishing, software, films – and in telecommunications. Our best education and training is globally competitive. You will not find examples outside the UK that are better than our best practice. But we have this long tail – the bottom 40 per cent is a real issue. When I was born, you got a good education to get a good job. That's now lost. The challenge is to build competitiveness and tackle exclusion and social breakdown."

In 1994, Yapp and colleague Malcolm Napier sat down and considered how technology could be used to re-design education to support lifelong learning. They came up with the idea of a networked learning community, that would 'deliver learning to the learner'. This was put into action as the South Bristol Learning Network – Maurice King's employer – which provided the impetus for more thought. Yapp says: "If you do everything bottom-up, the costs and the timescales are just impossible. I said to Malcolm: 'How would you help everyone to get involved in networked learning in the course of a single Parliament?' That's where we coined the concept of the National Grid. It was what the government could do to foster 1000 flowers blooming, and enable everyone to join in quickly."

In the same way as electricity is distributed from power stations to customers, says Yapp, the idea of a grid for learning was to make online learning resources available to libraries, offices, schools and homes over a national network. He says: "The lifelong learner attached to the grid might be 3, 10 or 80 years old. The learner is a both a student and a teacher – think about the case of two 5-year-olds showing each other how to do something, for example. At other times, he or she could also be an academic supporter, such as a librarian, or a researcher or assessor. Roles change from minute to minute." Meeting all these needs is the challenge, and he argues: "The content, not the infrastructure, must drive the change."

He says: "Computers started off in science and engineering in the Forties and Fifties. In the next 20 years, they reached commerce and government. The largest sector of the economy that is largely untouched by technology is culture and learning. Digital museums and libraries, schools and colleges are relatively new and untapped, so there is a push from the market to adopt technology. The question is: Does technology win out – or society?"

❷ Starting at Home

RON Culley confesses that when he bought his home computer, he had no idea how it worked. "I thought that someone sprinkled fairy dust inside the machine to make things happen," he laughs. A year later, Ron admits that some of the fairy dust has rubbed off on him. Inspired by a computer-based encyclopedia, the 47-year-old Glaswegian, a self-confessed 'ordinary guy', has just completed his first novel. Like many people, Ron, who runs a development company, was apprehensive about buying his machine. "I thought I was being extravagant," he says. The breakthrough came when he began to explore *Encarta*, an all-singing, all-dancing encyclopedia from Microsoft. He was entering the world of multimedia. Unlike a book, this breed of encyclopedia had sound and motion – film clips, famous speeches, poetry recitals. And no matter where Ron started, he could dive in and follow a whole chain of links between different topics that he didn't even know were related. He says: "Suddenly, I realised you could identify a piece of information and let it draw you to other sources, without knowing where the next idea would lead. It was like a voyage of discovery."

▲　　▲　　▲

Ron became fascinated by the American Kennedy clan and their political careers. From the comfort of his armchair, he toured Boston and Dublin, learned of the exploits of the Mafia, listened to the words of statesmen. "Charmed and impressed" by his new-found skills and knowledge, he decided to write a novel. Nine months and 80,000 words later, his book, *The New Guard,* an international adventure thriller, has been taken on by a literary agent. "Everyone says they have a book in them," says Ron. "But for me, the computer made it happen. I had two things that Ian Fleming didn't have. He needed to visit places to get local colour, but I only had to click a button. And when I wanted to alter the plot, I could simply move the text around on the screen, rather than having to start again."

THE RISE AND RISE OF THE PC

Not everyone plans to tackle the blockbuster novel, but, like Ron Culley, more and more people are investing in personal computers (PCs). According to the latest figures from research firm IDC, 5.6 million households – 26 per cent of households in Britain – now own a machine. As the Stevenson report on information and communications technology in UK schools pointed out, there are now many more computers in British homes than in schools. More than anything else, it is the incredible rise in popularity of the home computer that has been responsible for raising the profile of technology and the role it can play in learning.

Today's personal computer is an impressive beast. The understated-looking machine on the kitchen table is more powerful than the enormous computer that first sent Man to the Moon, and it is set to keep on getting cleverer. Multimedia technology is improving all the time, and so software designers and home users alike can use high-quality images, sound and video to add interest to even the most mundane of tasks. Thanks to dramatic progress on developing software that recognises the human voice, many people are now talking to their computers. Dictating letters without having to bother with the keyboard will become a standard method of use in future.

For many families, the main motivation for making a major investment in one of these powerhouses is their children's future, even though they are not always sure exactly how the machine will help. In a recent survey by computer manufacturers Packard Bell, one parent said: "There is pressure on parents to buy a computer for the children; performance at school and their future careers depend on it. The earlier they get used to them, the more advanced they become." Another said: "It is not just the children who put the pressure on. Other parents flaunt PC ownership as though it was a mark of good parenting."

But thanks to the pressure, a whole generation of digital kids are now confident computer users when they arrive at school, and they enjoy the luxury of being able to type essays or research projects without having to queue for the school machines. Their parents are also targets for a huge range of children's software aimed at education. Much of it is 'edutainment' that combines entertainment with learning, often through drill-and-practice: solve this equation correctly and you may zap an invader; name the founder of the English Navy and you can sink a Spanish galleon. Many titles boast, quite rightly, that they are linked to the school curriculum, although the type of unsupported claims made by some vendors would not be tolerated in other types of retailing. For children, especially those brought up in front of screens and well-used to zapping, edutainment can be a captivating, and even educational experience, but the real potential of home software lies elsewhere.

As in Ron Culley's case, some of the most fascinating learning takes place almost by accident, and from unexpected sources. Children who play sophisticated adventure games, for example, tend to buy the accompanying book that reveals the tips and short-cuts for success. The desire to win the game motivates the youngster to master these dense and complicated volumes, often deemed to be way above the child's reading age. And the vogue for fantasy football games has led to a whole raft of six-year-olds who, thanks to their trade in top players, are adept at counting in millions. But the real joy of multimedia is that it gives the whole family opportunities to discover new ways of learning – and to explore, perhaps for the first time in their lives, what holds most appeal.

Many people in the educational world are familiar with the theory of 'multiple intelligences', developed in the early Eighties by Dr Howard Gardner, professor of education at Harvard University. Although intelligence has been traditionally measured by a standard IQ test, Gardner has identified eight different kinds of intelligences. These range from the capacity to use and understand language, through the ability to represent the spatial world in the mind, to the ability to relate to other people. Different people, says Gardner, have different combinations of these intelligences, and they respond in different ways to different kinds of content, such as language, music or other people. Armed with a PC, anyone – even someone deemed to have a learning disability – can explore what works for them. Would it be better to listen to a narrative on life in Caesar's time, or to take a 3D tour of the streets of Ancient Rome? Adults and children alike can walk round the inside of an atom, build a steam locomotive and watch it chug across the screen, hear an essay read out as it is being typed on the keyboard. Even children who don't respond well to aural information are learning to play the piano by hitching a musical keyboard up to a computer and having the musical signals converted to moving images on the screen. Play smoothly, and a carousel spins beautifully with the rhythm; make a mess of it, and the jerky movements show immediately where the problems lie.

The home learning centre of the future will help people assess how they learn, and direct them to suitable materials of all kinds; software, books, broadcasts, toys, do-it-yourself kits. Often this will not even call for a trip to the shops, thanks to the other key factor in the educational technology revolution – the Internet.

100 MILLION ON THE NET

Today, almost 100 million people around the world are connected to the Internet. They use this remarkable network of computer networks to make new friends, find long-forgotten ancestors, check up on cricket scores, analyse pictures from Mars, take degrees, play chess, read the newspapers, collaborate on school projects and major international research, diagnose their own illnesses, buy a host of goods from flowers to ferrets and send proposals for everything from car insurance to marriage. It was not always like this. The worldwide network of computer networks grew from an exercise in 1969 to link computers at four American universities so that they could share information. More computers were added, and 'internetting' technology developed so that networks which had been built in different ways could easily talk to each other. Universities and researchers around the world quickly realised the value of the Internet for communicating and sharing data, although it still took considerable technical prowess to be able to achieve it.

The Internet remained largely the province of universities and computer boffins until the early Nineties, when its public face was radically overhauled with the arrival of the World Wide Web. Before the Web, information appeared as reams of text, and only those who were *au fait* with the inner workings of the network could find it. Today, people can explore the Web in much the same way as Ron Culley explored his multimedia encyclopedia, diving in and following a chain of related topics – often accompanied by pictures, videos and music – at the click of a button.

The wonder of the Internet – and its critics suggest, its weakness – is that it is still a massive free-for-all. Anyone with a properly-equipped computer or television set and access to a phone line can be online, connected, taking part in the action. A small fee not only buys access to the Web, but also an address for electronic mail, or e-mail. This is the passport to being able to send electronic messages to any other e-mail user in the world, in a few minutes and for the price of a local phone call. If that is not fast enough, there is always Internet Relay Chat, whereby people hold conversations by typing messages back and forth as they sit at their screens, or even Internet telephony, which enables Internet users armed with the right software to actually talk to one another via their computers, a cheaper option than making a conventional telephone call.

The Internet has grown organically; no-one owns it, no-one is in charge and there is no pecking order. Anyone is allowed to publish information on the Web, and the casual browser is likely to find pictures from Mrs McShuggle's family album rubbing shoulders with slick marketing material from multi-million-dollar corporations. Although they may not be aware of it, most people who have come to terms with a multimedia computer have the skills needed to build a collection of Web pages, and their Internet Service Provider – the organisation responsible for connecting them to the Internet – can usually help turn their efforts into a Web site, complete with its own address, and make it available to the world.

Fans say the Internet is an indispensable treasure trove of information: a vast library, a source of knowledge and expertise available any time, anywhere. How else could a student read about his subject in distant universities or labs which he was not even aware existed? Or an eight-year-old put questions to a NASA scientist about her school project? And where else can most people go for in-depth information on scientific developments that move too fast for conventional publishing? Certainly not to the shelves of the library.

Critics counter that the Web is a vast vanity publishing house and that many hours can be wasted aimlessly 'surfing' useless information. Even a request to one of the search engines for references to a seemingly narrow topic can turn up thousands of Web sites to investigate. Typically, schools have got round the problem by connecting to the

Internet via a specialised service such as as RM Internet For Learning and BT's CampusWorld. These provide signposts to useful, vetted Web sites plus additional information, without the need to venture out onto the more obscure and sometimes unsavoury corners of the Web. Internet service provider AOL provides a similar link for families at home. New technology is also coming to the rescue. Search engines are being superseded by software agents, or knowbots. Programmed to a user's interests, an agent can constantly seek out sites that fit the 'shopping list' while the user is asleep or even on holiday.

But the Internet's future lies not only in its ability to deliver information to the learner's door, but also for its potential to bring together groups of teachers and learners to work together on ideas and projects, and to build and share their material. Today, some of the most exciting developments underway in all fields of education involve collaboration over the Internet. They are taking place not only in schools, colleges and universities, but at companies, football grounds, old folk's clubs and in the High Street.

THE NEW LITERACY

Technology is permeating nearly every aspect of life and work, and citizens of the future who lack technology skills will be at a severe disadvantage. Confidence with ICT is part of the New Literacy for the 21st century. In a speech to Commonwealth education ministers, Education and Employment Minister Baroness Blackstone said: "We are regarding the development of children's information and communication technology skills as the fourth 'R', a basic skill as important as literacy and numeracy." Training, and access to computers and the Internet is becoming essential for everyone – and there are fears that segments of the population will be left out, either because they can't afford equipment, or they believe they simply won't be able to master the skills.

Some experts have suggested that as multimedia takes over the screens, reading and writing will become much less important. But according to Ray Barker of the National Literacy Association (NLA), with the rise of the Internet, literacy is becoming more essential than ever. He says: "The Internet is heavily text-based. People say: 'Isn't it wonderful, children can deal with the Internet?' But they can't, because they are being faced with enormous amounts of text, often not appropriate for their age level. And on the Internet, text no longer has a linear structure – it is possible to start off somewhere, go somewhere else, then somewhere else, and never come back to your basic idea. Research has shown that only 25 per cent of people come back to the page where they began. Whether that is going to change the notion of narrative and what structure is, or whether it is just going to cause a mess, I don't know – there is a whole area that has to be researched on how people read text on screen. But anyone without basic functional literacy is going to find it enormously difficult because they are never ever going to get through to the end of something. E-mail is also changing the whole nature of written style, because when people write e-mails they write in a completely new way. So computers are changing literacy, but I don't think they are changing the need for basic functional literacy."

A frightening number of people risk being left behind. The latest Literacy Survey by the Office of National Statistics reveals that one in five British adults has problems with reading, writing and numeracy. According to the NLA, Britain has always had a problem: every year, 16 per cent of youngsters leave school with poor literacy, and this figure has remained constant for 50 years, no matter which method of teaching has been in vogue or which government has been in power. But the literacy demands of society have increased dramatically. *Literacy Skills for the Knowledge Society*, the report from the OECD, points out that half of all adults in the United Kingdom, although they read and write, 'have problems using the complex information that they are likely to encounter at work, at home and in the community at the end of the 20th century'. The report, which grades literacy on five levels, goes on to say that most of the OECD countries surveyed had a similar proportion of people who couldn't cope with complex information, but the UK had noticeably the largest numbers of adults at both the lowest and highest levels of competence.

Closing this yawning gap at an early stage is being given top priority in schools. Literacy schemes are underway, and 1998 has been designated the Year of Reading. The tricky problem of helping adults with literacy – complicated because of the stigma and embarrassment involved – is being tackled by the Basic Skills Agency, in a number of imaginative initiatives which cover home and work.

The Agency was responsible for developing the Family Literacy initiative, which encourages parents and their young children (3-6 year-olds) to learn together at short courses run in schools. Courses are now being run by 33 local education authorities, and will be extended to include older children. The scheme was in initially piloted in Cardiff, Liverpool, Norfolk and North Tyneside, where results were independently monitored. Charlotte Pearson of the Basic Skills Agency says: "The most recent research suggests amazing results. None of the parents had any kind of qualifications or education, but after finishing the course, 60 per cent went on to another course. And that's apart from the results for the children. It is giving the parents an excuse to come in and get help because they are doing it for their children."

The Agency, which has spent five years working with large companies to increase employees' basic skills, is now planning to use computers in a new project to help smaller organisations. Charlotte Pearson says: "Small firms seem to be more likely to employ people who have basic skills difficulties, and small firms are going to be employing an increasing number of people. They also find it difficult to send employees away on courses, so it is hard to get any training, let alone basic skills." The approach is not to run courses, but to subtly incorporate training into work. For employees who use computers, one plan is to build additional help into everyday software. So when someone calls up advice on how to fill in a company form, for example, help with spelling and punctuation will also be available. And for those who don't already use computers, the software can be used to offer basic skills training under the guise of learning about ICT.

Charlotte Pearson says: "People are very happy to say they can't use computers, but not happy to admit they can't read or understand a form. This is a way of reaching them from a different angle. All our research suggests that literacy needs are becoming greater because of the way that work is changing with the use of information technology. We have done studies that show there are hardly any jobs that don't need a foundation level of literacy and numeracy. Just look at the use of statistical process control in manufacturing – even being on a production line in a factory you can't get away without having literacy and numeracy skills."

③ Schools: Exploding the Myths

WHEN it is time for an art lesson at Port Charlotte Primary School on the Scottish island of Islay, budding Picassos take out their paints and paper and settle down to work, under the watchful gaze of their art teacher. As the pictures progress, she offers encouragement, advice and maybe even a demonstration of colour mixing or brush techniques. An idyllic, old-fashioned scene – except that the teacher is 100 miles away from the school, on the other side of the county. She and her young charges are working together with the help of video cameras and computers.

▲   ▲   ▲

Both teacher and pupils work in front of videoconferencing screens – computers incorporating tiny video cameras which film the action, and relay it over a high-speed communications link to the viewer's computer screen, where it appears in much the same way as a TV picture. This sounds like a complicated way of teaching children a subject which has been achieved perfectly well by traditional means for centuries, but the high-tech equipment is part of a ground-breaking project, which could point to a major revolution in the way schools organise themselves in future.

Were it not for the new technology, the youngsters at remote Port Charlotte would miss out on a full education. With only 30 pupils, the school supports three teachers, who are jacks of all trades. Full-time specialist teachers are out of the question, and the costs of sending a visiting expert to such an out-of-the-way spot – often involving a day's round trip for a half-hour lesson – are prohibitive. The school is not unique: in its local area of Argyll and Bute alone, there are 98 other rural primaries. Most are isolated, with one or two teachers, and some have as few as four pupils.

In 1991 the local council decided to confront the problems of distance, time and shrinking budgets. They began, not with technology, but with a simple plan that allowed schools to pool their resources. Carol Walker, head of development services for the council, sat down in her Oban office with a road map and a pencil, and clustered the schools into co-operatives – groups that would share teachers, materials and funds. Modern technology made the scheme work. "We realised that if we wanted schools to share, we had to give them communications," she says. The first step was to introduce cordless phones, allowing staff in single-teacher schools to spend more time in the classroom. Fax machines offered a quick and easy way for pupils to share and compare work.

Next step was to investigate the use of electronic learning material, which any school could use with the aid of a computer and telephone line. At first, pupils were allowed access to the Internet, but the results were not encouraging. The children spent too much time surfing, looking at anything that caught their attention, rather than turning up useful material. So the council decided to hire teachers to build online learning material, which was made available on its own network, Argyll Online. The service provides projects and reference materials that incorporate the best of the Internet. It enables pupils to e-mail chums from other schools, and teachers to take part in online conferences about the curriculum and day-to-day administration.

The introduction of videoconferencing was a major breakthrough, allowing face-to-face, instantaneous communication. For children in schools such as Port Charlotte, it has become as familiar a part of their classroom life as the blackboard. They use it to practise their language skills, speaking French and Gaelic to youngsters at other schools. They learn mathematics and music from faraway tutors, even staging on-screen concerts to distant music teachers. And before they make the daunting move to a large, often distant secondary school, 11-year-olds from tiny villages videoconference together, making friends in preparation for the big day. "The results have been remarkable," says Sally Fulton, head teacher at Port Charlotte. "Communication with the wider world has completely broadened the children's horizons."

In addition to running schools and taking full-time classes, which often span different age groups, Sally and the other teachers have had to come to terms with new teaching techniques, and master the technology on which so much classroom activity now depends. But the benefit of the co-operative arrangement is that they have an incentive to help each other. A network of teachers – called the Macnetters, as most of their computers are Apple Mac machines – offer advice and keep one another up to date. Teachers also have extra motivation, as the Argyll and Bute scheme saves them precious time and effort. With access to purpose-built course material, aimed at local schools, they don't waste hours re-inventing the wheel. They can also co-operate with their counterparts without leaving the classroom. Sally Fulton says: "If I attend a meeting, I would have to leave the school the day before, and return two days later. I can see that the community will be involved in coming to the school. Rather than attending meetings, especially in the winter when it is difficult to travel, they can come here and use the equipment in the evenings."

"I have been told that we are further ahead than anyone else in the world," says Carol Walker, and she is probably right. Even city-based schools, which until recently would never have contemplated distance learning, are beginning to admit they could learn a lesson from these rural teachers about getting together and using technology to make pared-to-the-bone budgets stretch further. With fast, cheap access now offered to every school, the Argyll and Bute experience could be attainable for everyone.

Few children are as familiar with technology as these rural youngsters. Some schools are still saving supermarket vouchers and running jumble sales in the hope of being able to buy a computer, and staff are considering the tricky problem of how to run a cable from the only phone line, in the headmaster's office, to connect classrooms to the Internet. The latest figures available from the Department for Education and Employment (for 1996) showed that there were 19 pupils for every computer in primary schools, and nine in secondary schools. These are not all whizz-bang multimedia models – many computers date back to the mid-Eighties – and even some of the brand-new machines sit unused in classrooms or unwrapped in store cupboards.

FANS AND CRITICS

But all this is set to change with the arrival of the National Grid for Learning. By 2002, all 32,000 schools in Britain will be connected free to the Internet, which they will be able to use for around £1 per pupil per year. Good-quality software will be specially developed and kitemarked for schools. Government and private funds are to be found for some computers – thanks to economies of scale, equipment should cost less anyway – and National Lottery funds are earmarked for training the country's half a million teachers to use them. Over nine million schoolchildren will be able to enjoy learning materials on tap, and use their own e-mail addresses to talk to the world. Which stimulates the question: what are they going to do with all this?

As plans for the Grid take shape, the debate about computers in the classroom has become heated. Teachers, parents, educational experts and casual observers are split over whether technology is a good or bad thing. While sceptics admit that children need computer skills to be able to survive in the modern world, they say that other than that, computers in schools are just a distraction. "All wired up. Now I can be as thick as an American" screamed a headline in *The Observer* (5 Oct, 1997), in an article claiming that high-tech experiments in American classrooms had failed, leaving dumbed-down children who were reliant on machines. There are fears that computers make things too easy – the same kind of arguments that surrounded the introduction of calculators in the Seventies. Dr Jeremy Dunning-Davies, a lecturer in Mathematics at Hull University, laments the fact that some of his undergraduates arrive unable to do long division; at school it wasn't considered necessary to teach them, because they would always be armed with calculators. He asks: "What are the schools going to do with all these computers? What is going to make up for the teacher hearing each child read every day?"

Nick Seaton, chairman of The Campaign For Real Education, a group of parents and teachers that campaigns for higher standards in state education, takes a more moderate stance. "Computers are marvellous – we aren't worried about them being used in schools," he says, "but if they take over to too large an extent, they could undermine learning about the basic subjects and the use of books. You can buy a lot of books for the price of a computer. Maybe one or two periods a week using computers – and great for out-of-school clubs – but not too much in the normal school day."

Both fans and critics of technology put forward some valid arguments, but the point is that technology is neither a good nor a bad thing in itself. The important thing is how it is used, and that will determine whether the schools of the future make a success of it. Shirley Venneema and Howard Gardner sum up the idea in their paper,

Multimedia and Multiple Intelligences when they say: "Technology does not necessarily improve education. Take a simple innovation like the pencil – one can use it to write a superlative essay, to drum away the time, or to poke out someone's eye." A number of projects, often made possible by a combination of public funds and help from computer and communications companies, have begun to dispel some popular myths, and reveal how the classroom of tomorrow could look.

THE MOTIVATION FACTOR

In London's Docklands, over half of all schoolchildren speak a language other than English at home – any one of 75 different languages. It is a low-income area, where 42 per cent of families have more than four children, and one in every five pupils is from a single-parent family.

In 1995, the National Literacy Association teamed up with the London Docklands Development Corporation in a two-year effort to raise standards of literacy by working with seven- and eight-year-olds, a total of 600 children in 15 schools. The London Docklands Learning Acceleration Project took an unorthodox and sometimes controversial approach to the problem, with fascinating results.

As far as technology was concerned, there were two separate strands to the project. The first was to give each child an Acorn Pocket Book, a tiny £200 computer which would help with writing. It contained a word processor for producing text, a spreadsheet for gathering and analysing data, a spelling checker and thesaurus – much the same kind of software you would find on a home computer being used to run a small business – plus some additional word games. There was no multimedia – a deliberate decision, says Ray Barker of the NLA, who ran the project. "Teachers expected some sort of content, like a CD-ROM, that would keep children happy. But a Pocket Book doesn't have anything like that on it; you have to do something with the system. If you watch children with CD-ROMs, they often click a great deal and then print a few things. I am not a great believer that there any great learning experiences going on there."

The idea was that children could take their machines home, to continue with writing projects they had begun in school. Ray Barker says: "To a lot of schools this was a shocking suggestion – the assumption was that the machines would be stolen." During the course of the project, however, only 10 machines were lost, thanks to some cunning on the part of the project team.

The plan was to have an adult accompany children home with their computers – a challenge, given that parents were reluctant to come to school, even on parents' evenings. Ray Barker says: "We worked underhandedly with the kids, letting them use the machines until they absolutely loved them, then we took them away and said: 'You're not going to get these until somebody comes and signs a document saying they are going to come to school and escort them home'. So, of course, we had a 100 per cent attendance of parents." Children were able to show them on the spot what they could do with the computers, and convince their parents that they were valuable and needed to be protected.

Similar techniques had also been employed to encourage teachers to take part. "During the first term of the project," says Ray Barker, "the teachers were finding it very difficult to deal with the technology, and they were backing off. So we decided to train all the children individually. They made their teachers' lives a misery until the teachers were able to use the system. We really had to move it along, and show teachers that the children were able to use the system and they shouldn't be afraid of it."

The youngsters' reaction to their new machines is best illustrated by this excerpt from one of the reports on the project: 'The teacher assured us that Nicholas could not write. He was one of the most easily distracted and distracting children in the class. But he was curious about the Pocket Book and gave the impression of reluctantly following the group session. The five children were learning how to use the 'Write' word processing facility on the machine and recording their findings at the same time. To give the writing a purpose and to facilitate the use of the tool, a part of the brief of our project, Nicholas decided to write a letter to the person he most wanted to help him that evening. Nicholas chose his grandad and wrote the following (final print-out): 'Dear Granddad, This is how you use it. Press on. All words comes up. If you want to write, use arrows. If you want to write to someone you put the name in. It's not a toy. Don't drop it. Press Acorn and S to save it.'

'He had worked for two sessions of 30 minutes (with a break for assembly and play) and chose not to work with his usual support teacher. He was thrilled with his success in class, and even more so the next day, after he had taught his grandad at home and corrected his mistakes with him. The writing was brought back to school, downloaded on to a classroom desktop machine, edited again, printed and displayed.

FOUR THINGS HAD HAPPENED HERE:

❑ **A seven-year-old had used a piece of sophisticated equipment (usually associated with City businessmen) in order to write for a real purpose.**

❑ **He had achieved success in moving through all the stages of the writing process (for once).**

❑ **He had changed his status at home by introducing new technology and showing himself an expert.**

❑ **He had confounded the expectations of his teacher, his family and himself!'**

Results showed that the children became more motivated to write, and more confident writers. Rather than sitting staring at a blank sheet of paper, terrified that they were going to make a mistake, they could use the word processor to begin drafting ideas, and revise their work at leisure until they were happy with it. One of the most rewarding moments must have been when a group of seven-year-olds decided that the instruction manual supplied with the machines was inadequate, and so re-wrote it. The computers were used to write about topics ranging from religious education to science, and taken on field trips to help in the recording of findings. In keeping with the one of the aims of the project – to link new technology to traditional approaches to literacy – children were encouraged to keep electronic diaries of the books and magazines they read, and interview their friends about their reading habits. Parents, many of whom joined in on the writing at home, were invited to come along to basic skills workshops at schools and libraries. Over the course of two years, local libraries reported an increase in membership and a rise in borrowing.

FAREWELL TO THE TEACHER?

The other unorthodox use of computers in the Docklands project involved integrated learning systems (ILSs). An ILS is a software program that guides a learner through a subject at his or her own pace. It is designed to work interactively, monitoring progress and setting tasks or tests on the basis of how the learner is progressing, without the need for a teacher to intervene. This kind of software is more common in American schools than in British, where the jury is still out on its effectiveness. A long-running study carried out by the British Educational Communications and Technology Agency (BECTA, formerly the National Council for Educational Technology) on how ILS can help maths and literacy has so far concluded that some systems can help maths, but has seen few direct gains in literacy attributable to this way of learning. Two groups of children progressed most in maths: very able pupils and under-achievers. Thanks to ILS, there has been much speculation that in the schools of tomorrow, computers will replace teachers.

The system used in the Docklands classrooms was 'open' – it could be influenced by teachers, who could alter the pace or set targets. However, the children were given the power to set their own targets and report on their own progress. "We started doing this because the reporting procedures on the system were useless," says Ray Barker. "The graphs it produced were totally incomprehensible, so we had to find a simpler way of doing it. There is nothing simpler than starting from the children's perspective."

While they were using the computer, children were being given responsibility for their own learning, and could clearly see how they were progressing. At the end of each session, they would record their own progress on simple forms ('I got less than 92% in these words and I had to do them again. The second time round I wanted to be quicker.'). Knowing the teacher would be looking at the records and using them as the basis for other activities, pupils saw the computers as part of classroom work and not just as an excuse to 'play' unsupervised.

Results were encouraging: after one year, some schools had made leaps in reading skills of up to 19 months. But the most intriguing finding was that technology seemed to be acting as a leveller: children whose first language was not English were learning at the same rate as the other children. "They were still behind, but they were now learning at the same pace," says Ray Barker. "It was the same with children who qualified for free school meals. Those children would be put down as socially disadvantaged and therefore would be expected to learn more slowly.

"One of the things about low expectations of children in inner city areas is that they are given work which people think is appropriate to them. It is not a criticism of teachers – they have to manage children working at all different levels, and therefore to give some people fairly simple work is fine. But the computer does not make judgements, it does not have expectations. A managed learning system says: 'You can do this. If you can't do it, we'll take you back and we'll teach you how to do a bit more'. It says: 'Carry on, well done, well done'. It doesn't say: 'No, you can't do that, we'll have to give you lots of easier work, so sit in the corner and colour in this picture'. It doesn't matter who you are, what you are, where you are – that's the magic of it."

Where does this leave teachers? Certainly not out of work. As Barker points out, his project proved that this kind of system can be successful, but he doesn't claim that it is a panacea – not even in the sphere of literacy, an area of desperation where people feel there must be 'an answer'. New technology will create work for teachers, as it can only be successful if it is part of an overall classroom approach that is carefully planned and executed. The Docklands experiment shows that teachers will have to adapt their teaching methods, and it will challenge some of the fundamental ideas that they themselves learned long ago. But, as the piece of paper pinned to a project office wall in East London says: 'If you always do what you have always done, you always get what you always had.'

CONFIDENT LEARNERS

The potential rewards are borne out by another project, the £4 million Bristol Education Online Network, begun in 1996. Jointly funded by BT and ICL, BEON created an electronic community of nine primaries, one secondary and one special school in a deprived area of Bristol, which were linked by high-speed networks. The networks gave everyone access to a variety of resources – CD-ROMs, the Internet, videoconferencing and integrated learning systems for maths and English, plus advice and training for teachers on how to use the material. The goal was to assess the value of these for pupils and teachers.

At one of the schools, Whitehouse Primary in South Bristol, Head Teacher Anthony Austin is quite clear about the challenges he faces: "In our area, children have very low expectations of what they can do. A number of eight- or nine-year-olds have said to us quite bluntly: 'I am going to go straight on to the dole.'" Since BEON began, he says, the children's attitude to work has improved significantly: they do more, and their work is better planned, organised and thought out. "Children who before would give up very quickly, now feel good about what they are going to produce and so they have developed more stickability. They now do research at home and bring things back into school – that might be normal in middle-class schools but it is not normal for us. Their self-esteem has also risen. Using technology has raised their sights – they believe that they have employment possibilities because they are skilled."

However, this is not all down to the fact that they are sitting in front of screens – the teachers are making a major contribution, says Austin. "It is very easy to go into a classroom to see children 'busy' on computers when nothing is actually happening. We have done a huge amount of development work ensuring that the children have very clear frameworks within which to work, which support them initially and then become the framework that they use naturally. Having a very clear structure and progression is part of the success."

Even though Austin says it is probably due to a combination of factors, some children at Whitehouse have made dramatic leaps in their reading ages of between two and three years in a single year. But when it comes to sitting standard attainment target (SAT) tests, one of the quirky things is that standards at Whitehouse hardly appear to have risen at all. Austin says: "We consider that English work has improved dramatically. But we spend a lot of time training children to ask pertinent questions and then to develop work from those questions and use them to interrogate text. The SAT tests just present them with a big booklet, with a list of someone else's questions that they haven't been involved in putting together, and a piece of text that has no useful meaning to them other than it is an exercise that they have got to do. Some of our work has very usefully helped children with their basic study skills at a very high level, but when it comes to jumping through the hoops of a national test, it hasn't really helped in that regard at all. But it depends on what you consider to be the more worthwhile learning – to provide the youngsters with lifelong study skills, which will never leave them, or teach them to jump through a comprehension test."

Several schools in BEON also found that, as children learned new-found skills and their confidence increased, traditional barriers broke down, and pupils began to help one another, and even teachers. "They see themselves as having a particular expertise to share with another child or teacher who is feeling insecure about a piece of work," says Austin. This represents a fundamental shift in the traditional teacher-pupil relationship. To some teachers, it may constitute loss of control, and a severe threat. But, largely due to the introduction of technology, it has already started to happen in many classrooms anyway. As one parent who works in the educational technology field is embarrassed to admit: "My son's teacher can't work the class computer – she can't even get it to print anything. When it breaks down, Adrian has to fix it – and he's nine years old."

Anthony Austin says: "To us, the computer mouse is just a pencil." Evidence suggests that as technology becomes commonplace, and teachers are helped to get to grips with the technicalities, they will then have to come to terms with new teaching methods, new ways of assessing pupils and new ways of relating to their classes. Judging by the BEON experience, many may also have to cope with the shock of having a newly-motivated breed of pupil who turns up early at school, has to be turfed out by the caretaker at 5 o'clock, and is eager to learn. One lad, encouraged by the information he had found online to make a rare visit to the library, even enthused to his teacher: "Do you know, sir – there is some information in books that isn't even on the Internet?"

The good news for beleaguered teachers: help is at hand, in the form of new managed services for schools. The BEON project trialled such a service, and it offered two benefits. First, it removed the hassle of having to worry about running a complicated ICT operation. Instead of giving the responsibility for technology to an overworked member of staff already trying to do a full-time teaching job and a thousand other things, schools could outsource the job to outside experts, in the same way as many companies do, leaving themselves free to concentrate on what they get paid for.

Colin Fletcher at Fulford, another of the BEON schools, says: "If you develop a whole teaching and learning style around computers for all lessons, then if the damn things don't work, you are really left high and dry. We can't afford to have the machines out for two days." Second, the service took advantage of the network to deliver training and advice to schools *in situ*, and helped them share their experiences.

When a whole group of schools and colleges are willing to join forces, this kind of scheme becomes affordable and commercially viable. The BEON service, provided by ICL and since packaged as the Knowledge Utility, is now being provided on a commercial basis to the Merseyside Education Online Network, a group of 10 schools and two training centres in Merseyside. One of the benefits of the National Grid for Learning will be to make managed services a more attractive option for all schools.

4 Schools: The Global Classroom

A project in North-East Scotland recently explored how an electronic network could be used to help able children develop their thinking skills. It was aimed at small rural primaries, where able children are often not stretched to their full potential – they are alone at the top of the class, their ideas unquestioned and unchallenged by other children. The STARS (Superhighways Team Across Rural Schools) project, which began in 1996 and ran for a year, linked 18 primaries and two secondary schools. Because schools were so small, singling out only able pupils – one or two children at most – taking part would have caused social problems, so others were included in school groups of four or five. The aim was to teach thinking skills through problem solving, promoting critical thinking, creative thinking and collaborative learning. Computer-based assignments, all with a Space theme, were published on Web sites called launchpads, and some projects involved doing research on the Internet.

▲　　▲　　▲

On some problem-solving exercises, the children had to come up with a single solution on behalf of their school, working together in their own group and reaching some consensus. To find the best solution, children had to argue their case and accept other people's point of view. Other tasks called for co-operation with other schools. Typical was the STARS Trek Space expedition, which involved completing a whole set of challenges from liftoff on Earth until arrival at a planet called Argosia, where the children found artifacts left behind by the Argosians. Schools had to work together to interpret the finds, recording and collating information on 200 items. Each day, the adventurers were assigned different roles: first they were scientists, then historians, then anthropologists. In each role, they had to produce a collaborative report on their findings, with the help of e-mail.

Jim Ewing, from the Northern College in Dundee, who ran STARS, sums up the main findings: "One idea was that children should listen to others and respect their contribution. That was definitely an outcome. At first they were disappointed when other people shot down their ideas, and it took some time before they understood that other people's ideas might be worth considering. They were learning, as they might not do in a small rural school, that there were other people around who were just as bright as, or brighter than, they were themselves.

"In small schools, which often have only one teacher for all ages, children are more responsible for their own learning, but on the STARS project, they became more aware of themselves as learners and more able to evaluate themselves. The able children took responsibility as group leaders and as co-ordinators with other schools. Their problem-solving became more systematic – they knew what to do first, what next – and there were distinct gains in their use of critical thinking skills. At first they would produce an answer that was way off target – just a thought that had come into their heads. Later, these thoughts may still have entered their heads, but they weren't promoted in communication with others."

Ewing was determined to avoid wasting time on unprofitable surfing, and came up with an exercise to encourage children to develop their searching techniques. The aim was to create a datafile on the animals on Earth for people from other planets. Before anyone went near the Web, a group of young volunteers was given the task of coming up with the headings that they would use to group information – habitat, statistics, food – and these formed the basis of their Web searches. At the STARS Web site, they had to search three launchpads for a link to another Web site which had over 40 pages of information about animals. Once they reached these pages, the children knew exactly what they were looking for.

Ewing himself took part in exercises, responding to the children's comments online, encouraging them to develop their ideas. The schoolteachers provided what Ewing calls the 'scaffolding' for encouraging the pupils to construct their own learning. They set projects in motion and helped with concepts and vocabulary – "We made no attempt to water anything down; if language was difficult, we left it." They also brought things together at the end, helping the pupils to register what they had learned from an exercise.

Despite the fact that it was logistically difficult to sustain the collaborative work – in a small school the entire complement of children might have to disappear for a swimming lesson at one time – teachers reported that the project awakened their professional interest in distance learning, in differentiation in teaching for different pupils, and in teaching thinking. Many of them began from a standing start, never having used technology before. "Some were seriously terrified, and some were seriously anti-technology," says Ewing. "The phone calls at the beginning were just pure terror. But I was able to say to them: 'I am learning as you are learning'. Now, I don't think there is a single 'anti' left."

He says: "I think there is a world of teaching thinking waiting to be awakened. I passionately believe that children need thinking skills more than ever before, but I am also rather disappointed that, except in a few pockets of excellence, the main run-of-the-mill teaching doesn't seem to have a great deal of attention for this." The main barrier, he says, is hard work. "You have to know what you are doing. The teachers were beginning to see what they were doing – if I or some system had been able to continue to support them, they would have shot ahead."

Funding for the STARS project has now dried up, but Jim Ewing says that he has dozens of ideas about how the STARS experience could be applied in other types of schools and for other children, including those who learn at home. It could also be used in industry, to help teach thinking skills, management techniques, and the ability to cope with change.

SCHOOLS AND THE NET

Some schools are seasoned Internet users; others are now only starting to take tentative steps on to the Net. At the beginning of 1998, only 6,000 of Britain's 32,000 schools had Internet connections. Thanks to the UK NetYear initiative, dubbed by prime minister Tony Blair 'The biggest public-private partnership in any education system anywhere in the world', this figure should rise to 17,000 by the end of 1998. UK NetYear's founders, Cisco systems, ICL, Sun Microsystems and the Telegraph Group, are kick-starting the National Grid for Learning with a promotional campaign that aims to rally round local communities and businesses to help equip and train schools, and a series of national projects that encourage schools to familiarise themselves with the Internet. ICL's David Wimpress, executive chairman of UK NetYear, says: "With an estimated 60 per cent of all computers in schools being out-of-date and the need to train 80 per cent of the UK's 450,000 teachers in the use of ICT, we have a huge challenge." The initiative is also offering a free e-mail address for life to every one of Britain's 10 million teachers and pupils.

Soon every school will be able to reach out and take part in the worldwide action. But in the global classroom of tomorrow, will children merely spend their time, as cynics suggest, dredging through material that is at best unsuitable, at worst downright harmful?

Experience shows that both teachers and pupils are smarter than their critics make out, as the country's largest Internet research project, Schools Online, recently revealed. With a total of £3.5 million funding from the Department of Trade and Industry and from 50 private sponsors, the project ran from 1995 to 1997. It gave 90 schools, mainly secondaries, the chance to find out what the Internet had to offer, and also gave pupils a taste of the technology they would be faced with in the workplace. Results showed that the Internet can not only act as a useful source of information, but that its ability to bring different groups of children together, both inside and outside the school walls, boosts their confidence and encourages them to feel greater responsibility for their own learning.

One of the main thrusts of the mammoth exercise was that children wouldn't just be let loose to look at 'interesting stuff' on the World Wide Web without a purpose. There were a host of different activities, but two of the main curriculum areas targeted were science and languages. Children were encouraged to take part in projects, working in teams with other schools, and to publish their own work on the Web. As 15-year-old Sophie put it: "The main thing is that you are actually taking part in the Internet, not just watching it go by."

She and her classmates in London seized the opportunity to use the facilities that the science project team had set up on the Schools Online Web site, to help with experiments that ranged from monitoring satellites to counting woodlice. She e-mailed teachers and children in other schools who were working on the same projects, asking for advice, and took part in online debates, in which other students helped her understand some of the equations she was having trouble with. Students doing research were directed to Web sites which had been critiqued in advance by the project team, so there were pointers to how relevant and useful the material was. "Often the books in the library are quite old, so the Internet helps you get up to date," said Sophie. There was an interactive laboratory, where schools could do experiments together and tell one another about their investigations. This tackled a classic problem in schools; it is usually tricky to draw conclusions from classroom experiments, because they produce such a small set of results. Add lots of data together, however, and young scientists stand more of a chance of coming up with valid theories. Indeed, there is no reason why classroom boffins shouldn't contribute to real scientific research in future, doing valuable field work – reporting on their local pond-life or climate, for example, as part of national projects.

A highlight of the Schools Online science area was 'ask a scientist' – a chance to find out what makes scientists tick by e-mailing questions to well-known figures. One of the most popular personalities was Britain's first astronaut, Helen Sharman. Many of the questions were predictable (How do you go to the loo in space?), but chatting to people like Helen – a chemist who had to master Russian, astronavigation, rocket theory and an intensive physical training programme before she shot into space – may have helped make science more accessible and fire children's enthusiasm for the subject. Budding star-trekkers could also receive live pictures from a robotic telescope on the Yorkshire Moors which is controlled from the Internet.

EXCITEMENT AND ACCESS

Many of the schools used their new-found ability to communicate with the world to improve foreign language skills. Children wrote to e-pals around the world, they read foreign newpapers on the Web and published stories that had been jointly written with their counterparts abroad. These activities are now becoming commonplace in today's classroom, where pupils are just as likely to practise their verbs with friends in Dunkirk or Denmark as they are with their teacher. And, rather than team up with, say, native French speakers, some schools level the playing field by finding partners who are also learning French as a second language, so that nobody feels insecure. One special needs class is even twinned with a class in Talinn, Estonia, that is learning English as a second language, so that both sets of children can support one another as they learn to read and write. At Linlithgow Academy in Scotland, secondary pupils doing Business Studies courses plan to link up with a Scandinavian school to run a real import-export business.

The Internet offers excitement and access to people and places that are otherwise beyond the reach of most children. Rural youngsters take 'virtual tours' around museum Web sites – not as good as the real thing perhaps, but not 500 miles away, either. And city-centre children who seldom make it beyond the 30 mph limit follow glamorous expeditions, e-mailing adventurers as they struggle across Polar ice floes or conquer Himalayan peaks. One of the most ambitious schemes is the annual Jason project, which takes schoolchildren from around the world on an 'electronic field trip' from the comfort of their computer screens. It is run by Dr Bob Ballard, discoverer of the Titanic, who set up the Jason Foundation after he was inundated by questions from schoolchildren about the technology he used to discover the wreck. Since 1989, children have followed the action on projects ranging from testing space exploration vehicles in Hawaii to studying tubeworms 6000 feet below sea level in the Sea of Cortez off Mexico. As communications have become smarter, the young viewers have been able to take a more active part in experiments; for example in a recent expedition to study life in coral reefs, they watched live underwater pictures which were transmitted to the expedition Web site via a ship and three satellite systems. Over the Internet, they could also take turns to manoeuvre an underwater robot.

Some material on the Internet is outstanding. The resources published by NASA are a good example. NASA's Volcano World site, for instance, provides visitors with a mountain of facts and figures, pictures, quizzes and games relating to the world's volcanos, the chance to be e-mailed every time a volcano erupts and the opportunity to put questions to prominent vulcanologists.

But even the good sites, although fascinating, may not always dovetail with the curriculum, many being designed for use in American schools. As they discover the limitations of the Web, teachers are beginning to join forces to build their own material. Web for Schools, an initiative funded by the European Union, is helping teachers across Europe to become Web authors. Since April 1996, 150 schools from 17 countries have been clubbing together to contribute information on topics ranging from energy to acid rain. A total of 750 teachers were first trained in the techniques in a whistle-stop tour of Europe, carried out by South Bristol Learning Network, the British partners in the scheme. After that, each school took responsibility for one subject, and others contributed, with some of the work now being done jointly by staff and pupils. Not only does the project broaden perspectives – one mathematics contribution, for example, was a survey of comparative living costs around Europe, calculated in ECUs – but it also helps share the burden. As one teacher says: "Every topic is so immense that nobody can be an expert in every facet of it." The National Grid for Learning should provide much more impetus for this kind of activity, and teachers will find themselves with very good reasons for learning to be Web authors.

DANGER ON THE INTERNET?

The Internet has been plagued with horror stories; a few clicks of a button, and children can stumble on any quantity of offensive and dangerous material, from pornography to recipes for bombs. There are undoubtedly seedy haunts out there. Like films, Internet sites may soon be given a rating, and there are already voluntary schemes that enable Web authors to classify their sites. Technically this is possible: the PICS rating system, developed by the WWW Consortium, which is responsible for coming up with technical standards for the Web, will allow sites to be labelled securely with a rating, or even some kind of quality kitemark or endorsement. But putting this into practice is a different matter. One man's terrorist is another man's freedom fighter, and finding a system that will satisfy a global audience is going to be an immense challenge.

A variety of safeguards are now operating in schools. Some schools use 'walled garden' Internet services, which allow access only to specified Web sites that have been checked out beforehand. Others use filtering 'nanny' software, popular in homes, which either monitors children's online activities, or actually prevents access to certain types of material and areas of the Internet, as well as preventing youngsters from sending out personal information to strangers. But increasingly, pupils are being offered a more grown-up option. They and their parents sign up to an honesty deal that commits pupils to behave responsibly. They understand that if they stray, they lose their Internet access. Most schools which operate this scheme report very few breaches of contract.

At Richmond Park School in Glasgow, headmistress Maggie Pollard takes a more pragmatic approach to the problem. The children use the Internet in an open area, always with another pupil and with staff nearby. Maggie says: "There haven't been any incidents of concern to date, but I think the reality is that the dangers are more transparent and upfront on the Internet. There is a lot of sense in fighting issues, but unfortunately they have to be discussed with young children nowadays. They need to develop caution and be aware of the traps they can be led into. At least with the Internet they have the power to throw the switch. It is harder to run away from someone in the street. The children live in the global world – that's their world, and they have a right to access it. Hopefully, through good education they will use it wisely."

LIFTING SELF-ESTEEM

Fulford School, the special school which took part in the BEON project in Bristol, caters for 11 – 16-year-olds whom other schools are no longer prepared to accept – most of them have been excluded from at least two schools. They have a range of abilities, and a variety of problems. One child has lived in 42 different homes. Head teacher Colin Fletcher says: "It is difficult to concentrate on school when you are not sure where you are going to be living tonight. We have a number of children who are quite clever, but every pupil in the school is badly underfunctioning relative to their own abilities. They are very difficult kids. The whole idea here is to lift their self-esteem – convince them that they can compete with their peers in work and academic qualifications."

For the children, he says, the Internet has proved an incredible motivator. "Some go on to chat lines (Internet Relay Chat), e-mailing kids in America. Everyone on the Internet pretends they are 18 – I don't think there are any 16-year-olds left in America. The kids here pretend, too, and when I sit with them sometimes, they say: 'How do I spell this?', because they don't want to make themselves look stupid. For the first time in their lives they see some reason to be able to spell and use reasonable grammar. They are forever saying: 'Can you help me to read this?' Before that, they thought reading was some kind of punishment. They feel less threatened by the computer than by a book. Many of them are still learning to read, and the book has been a bad experience for them. This is something new they haven't failed at. Other kids get into Web sites. So when they go to reading lessons they think maybe it is worthwhile after all, because they can read the Web pages.

"One boy found the DisneyWorld Web site and entered a competition on the Toy Story page. We got a letter with a copy of the Toy Story reading CD. It said: 'Thank you very much for entering our competition, it was only for American pupils, but have a copy of the CD anyway'. He was the only person in the British Isles to have a copy. That's a kid who had a lot of problems in school. We were really pleased." Another boy produced a history of heavyweight boxing, entirely under his own steam. He spent hours researching Web sites, printing out information and putting the story together coherently, producing a huge volume.

"It was an amazing achievement," says Fletcher. "and the computers help to produce presentable work. With handwriting, if it isn't good, the children get angry, tear it up and chuck it in the bin."

Although classes are small – six to seven pupils at most – Fletcher says there are frequent rows. "Traditionally, children with emotional difficulties don't get on with each other. I teach science, and getting two children to do an experiment together is hard work. But when they sit at the computer, they help each other out and do things together in a way they don't normally do in the classroom. They are chuffed that for once they are at the forefront of education and not lagging behind, which is what special education has traditionally been. They go and see their friends at home and say: 'I use the Internet'. Our kids are a good example to prove what you can do in education, because everything they have gained is purely from school. In a comprehensive school, many children may have access to their parents' computers. I am sure not one parent here has access to a proper computer."

EQUAL OPPORTUNITIES

Maggie Pollard has "a passion for technology". She runs Richmond Park School, a special-needs primary where many pupils require nursing or therapy during the school day. The children include those with severe learning difficulties through to able learners, and many have impaired sight or hearing. The Internet has provided an opportunity for everyone to get involved in projects.

The school was introduced to e-mail 10 years ago, by a trust that helped children who couldn't speak. "I started it with two boys, who now have their own Web sites," says Maggie. "It really has been an incredible motivator for the children."

On a recent project to improve literacy, pupils partnered with 'buddies' at a mainstream school in Glasgow. One activity involved e-mailing an electronic adventure story back and forth between buddies, each writing a chapter in turn.

The children are adept 'Webmasters', who design and publish the school's Web site. Recently, they wrote about a local swan called Nettie, asking: 'What would she see in your country?' They were deluged with replies from all over the world.

"Everyone got involved, and we built relationships," says Maggie. "When we use the Internet, it has to have a purpose. We have to agree the importance of technology to children – it's their world and they are the workforce of tomorrow. And we have to understand its equalising effect, particularly for disabled people. More and more people are working from home using technology, and we see that as providing equal opportunities for the children. Once you see technology in that context, it is really easy to believe in it. Our staff have a shared vision: we all know where we are going and why we are going there. We are empowering the children by giving them access to the most powerful tool at their disposal which we think is use of computers in the classroom."

She says that at Richmond Park, computers are not a 'bolt-on', but an integral part of the syllabus. The aim is to use them to help children demonstrate a progression of skills as they move through school: "If we can't do that, then we are in the wrong job – that's without looking at league tables or target setting. It's just basic common sense."

Young children start with special software to help with early learning skills – left/right sequencing, hand-eye co-ordination, and cause and effect. As they progress, they are increasingly given content-free software that depends on their input to produce results. "This enables them to be creative thinkers – that's what's important in the use of technology – we don't want to it just to become a left-brain thing," says Maggie.

They use a predictive word processor, which encourages slow writers by attempting to complete words for them, best-guessing each word as it is being typed. Storybook Weaver software enables the children to produce their own reading books that mean something to them. As they become more skilled, pupils produce their own multimedia packages and publish Web pages.

They use videoconferencing to talk to other schools, to link to staff at the National Museum of Scotland who help with projects, and to keep in touch with their classmates in London's Great Ormond Street hospital, where many are frequent patients. "Videoconferencing is a marvellous equaliser – almost as great as e-mail," says Maggie. "It is visually selective – you don't see your whole wheelchair – and it has street-cred, because it is a television! Children who have been reticent to communicate, or unable to use the keyboard, have found that the videoconferencing gives them a voice. They are keen to show that they can talk confidently and send messages across the world."

The school spends 75 per cent of its budget on information and communications technology and developing staff in its use. Teachers not only attend courses, they also deliver them, and are sent on secondment to act as tutors in mainstream schools.

Maggie Pollard says: "Teachers learn with teachers and with children. If you are working in this school you are a learner no matter who you are. Once the teachers accept that, they don't feel threatened by other people. They don't say: 'They know more than me'. That is so important because that is what I want the children to leave here with: having learned how to learn. I want them to know the process of learning and how you learn – I really don't care whether it is the Vikings, the Romans or sums. That is the most valuable skill I can give them – if they can get that by seeing and understanding that their teachers are part of this process as well – that learning is a lifelong thing – then they are getting a very good role model."

SCHOOLS IN THE COMMUNITY

The National Grid for Learning will bring together many groups of people with an interest in schools, and with a wealth of knowledge that could be put to good use in the classroom. These include parents, community groups, voluntary organisations, training centres and libraries and museums, all of whom will be able to electronically link to schools in future, in a 'connected learning community'.

Already some pioneering schemes are underway. At Highdown secondary school in Reading, the school has built an information 'hub' which allows families to link to school from home. Thanks to help from Microsoft, ICL and cable communications company Telecential, more than 50 homes have links, allowing families to e-mail the school, and use school resources such as CD-ROMs and specially-built Web pages for homework. A surprise bonus has been the enormous value of the school link to parents, who are proving that lifelong learning is soon stimulated when pupils need help with interesting projects.

A major breakthrough has been the use of parent power to create course material using sources on the Web and their own expertise. Jasmine Marsh, whose daughters attend Highdown, says: "My group of parents allied itself to the geography department. My husband is a hydrologist, so it made sense to use his skills. He is posting Web pages for the sixth form. I have been looking for Web material on Japan and Europe for the younger children. I had never touched a computer before this project – I was one of the generation that slipped though the net." She says that the project gave her the motivation to learn about computers. "I wanted to build more skills so that I knew what the girls were looking at and how they were working. My daughters helped me – it's a bonus when you can teach your Mum something."

The project has also forged closer links between parents and the school. Instead of meeting only during a couple of formal evenings each term, parents and teachers now have instant communication via e-mail. Mrs Marsh says: "I have always kept up to date with the children's work, but this has brought me closer to the aims and plans of the school." Spurred on by the success at Highdown, Reading Borough Council now plans to link all 42 primary and secondary schools in the Reading district. Highdown School already has its own plan to get more of its own students involved. It has started to sell its resources to local businesses which need to train their staff in ICT, and is using the fees to buy more computers. And people without machines at home will be able to link in from libraries and museums.

Another community network is giving learners of all ages access to technology by inviting them into schools. The £2 million Staffordshire Learning Net was launched in Staffordshire in late 1997. Set up by the Staffordshire Local Education Authority and educational supplier Research Machines with BT, it will link all Staffordshire's 400 schools, plus colleges, universities and libraries. Blake High School, in Hednesford, is one of the schools operating as an open learning centre, welcoming adults who want to use its computers or take courses in the evenings. But pupils are also taking the chance to do some after-hours study. Heather Holyhead, the school's network manager, says: "Between four o'clock and six we run a cybercafe, where anyone can drop in and pay a pound an hour to use the Internet. We've had everyone here from mums to retired people, but a lot of pupils actually come in and pay their money to do their homework. They feel they get a lot of information from the Internet – and it really does boost their studies."

There is a plan to use the network as the basis for homework clubs involving parents and children, although so far most family groups have come along to check out Web addresses in games magazines. "We have a lot of Star Trek fans here," says Heather. "Sometimes our students are not very forthcoming about their hobbies, but when they are in front of a computer you can see what they are interested in – Star Trek or whatever. They talk to you about it and come alive." Evening activities, run by local colleges and community organisations, provide a way for the school to fund part of its ICT bill, which is also met by sponsors. In the longer term, the network will be used to link students to resources at other schools and further education centres. Dave Cheeseman of the education authority says: "When we don't have enough pupils in a school to justify teaching a subject – Latin, or some modern languages, for example – we could use videoconferencing to link pupils to a remote lecturer."

5 Schools: Preparing for the Future

THE Dalton School, on New York's Upper East Side, has spent most of this century keeping ahead of educational trends. And some of its pioneering work shows just how stimulating technology can be, particularly in such straightforward areas as e-mail.

▲ ▲ ▲

In Dalton's classrooms and in its 62,000-book library, a powerful combination of enthusiasm and money is showing how valuable the PC is in supporting today's teachers. Ever since its foundation in 1919, the Dalton School (originally called the Children's University School) has been progressive in attitude. Its philosophy has always been to question the conventional wisdom, which held that education was all about formal memorisation of facts.

Today it has 1,300 elementary and high school students and 200 teachers – constituting an élite private school, which uses its resources to encourage innovation. As Frank Moretti, former associate headmaster, now at Columbia University puts it: "How can we take a system that is driven from the top down, and acknowledge the individual? The progressive movement in the United States saw itself in that role – how can we accommodate the need to socialise so many immigrants with individual capacities?" And the answer seemed to be that it could be done, but in the places where it was successful the teaching was in the hands of charismatic leaders. "The moment they lost energy, the students didn't carry through," says Moretti.

Transferring his own enthusiasm from the charismatic to the technical, he has been in the forefront of computer-driven education. And Dalton has also led the way, sometimes in unconventional directions. The school made the front cover of *Time* magazine 20 years ago with the headline 'Dalton Gang invades multinational bank computer' after a group of pupils hacked their way into the system of a Canadian bank.

Moretti says: "I don't believe in a body of knowledge that everyone must have. I believe in a quality of experience that is intellectual and personal that everyone must have. The most successful people in the world are not people whose heads are jammed with facts – those are often the least creative people, but the most interesting are those who have the confidence and the ability to be analytic, and who have access to themselves. Your education should equip you not just to go out into the world like a soldier with a rifle, but it should also give you the ability to analyse why you would kill or not kill. Basically, I don't care that much about content. But for people who do like content, I talk about the experience they would like students to have with this content."

In 1982, Moretti was inspired by a visit to New York's Museum of Natural History where he saw children digging in a sandbox in which things were buried. When he mentioned this to third-grade students, he found they were really interested in early peoples. With the help of an archaeologist, he built an enormous box at Dalton, filled it with sand, and created a hunting site at four different levels for four different historic ages. He says: "If you found cartridges, for example, you had to do research to find out if they came from the 1950s or the 1880s.

"These were third-grade, 8-9 year olds. Teachers were afraid of it, but I said: 'All you have to do is think along with them. You are going to dig things up, catalogue them. Each object has to be put on a grid and then a map.' Twenty children did it the first time, with me and my two secretaries. It was an incredible success – kids who had never before been interested in reading were aggressively involved in the library because they had to work out what different objects were and what age they came from." The school hired a full-time archaeologist and more sandboxes were built, to provide a series of digs that ended with high school students going on a real excavation.

And so the thinking teacher's development of the sandbox was a computer simulation of an archaeological excavation, which Moretti called Archaeotype. With five networked computers, a program was created. "Click and the dirt moved from a square of the site on to a screen that would shift it. Either an object is left on the screen or where it was found. There were 200 objects, and every time you found an object you had to research it." The students were actively engaging in what educators call constructivist learning, in this case constructing their own knowledge of the past by piecing together the evidence and attempting to make sense of it.

"It has in it the same problem that all constructivist experiences have. It needs an adult who can't sleepwalk through the process. Teachers have to be able to put themselves in a position where they face the unknown – they have to show children what it is like to have something new to them, too. That's where you get a chance to demonstrate how you do analysis and think on your feet. You mustn't focus on the content, but focus all the time on whether the child is learning to think about how to analyse and construct ideas."

Moretti says: "The students actively went into the library, and were really pushing the librarians to provide them with info that they didn't know how to find – again, the adults being driven by the children. We also would tell the children about anyone in the school who might be helpful. So what the project did – and this is for people who feel that computers make children into loners – is it created a level of sociability, but productive sociability, that you would never find in a traditional school where children are being instructed through textbooks. These sixth-graders penetrated the educational and knowledge resources of the school – both human and hands-on – better than any group of children I have ever seen before, and they continue to do this.

"Why is this important to new technologies? It is my belief that one of the most powerful things that new technologies can do, is it can create unpredictability in the lives of educators. The introduction of unpredictability is a positive thing for someone who is a constructivist educator. New technologies have the capacity to create these extraordinarily rich environments that are going to require a kind of supervision and professorial presence that isn't intimidated by the complexity of the constant novelty."

VALUE OF E-MAIL

Dalton School has many advantages that mainstream schools lack. As Moretti points out, most of the children arrive with a head start, already linguistically competent, having learned the basics at home. There is also the question of money. Recent technology projects have been funded by a $4 million donation from Robert Tishman, a building magnate. He intended to leave the money in his will, but when he toured Dalton one day in 1989, the 82-year-old former pupil was so impressed by what Moretti had done with computers that he gifted the money on the spot. "This is a revolution in education," he said. "I want to support it now."

Few schools can hope for this kind of help, but encouragingly, some of the materials developed at Dalton have been taken on and used successfully in other very different classrooms. Moretti used Archaeotype in an elementary school in Chula Vista, one of the poorest districts of California, where the children spoke any one of seven different languages. The pupil/teacher ratio was 30/1, compared with around 8/1 at Dalton, but Moretti says that the project was just as successful as it had been in Manhattan. Today, much of his work at Columbia University's Institute For Learning Technologies is aimed at mainstream education. And some of his other projects past and present reveal the true potential of technologies that are now becoming commonplace in schools.

The first thing thing that was done with the Tishman gift was to link all the classrooms at Dalton with a high-speed network of computers, and this gave students the ability to talk to one another via e-mail. "I don't think any other technology is as valuable as e-mail," says Moretti. "E-mail is the place any school should start, because you can change the ecology of the school. It has far fewer of the limits of the traditional oral culture of the school or written correspondence. Education's biggest problem has always been the fact you bring people together by force (the adults feel that too) in the classroom and then hope they will have stimulating, honest conversations. The most powerful thing we discovered was how the e-mail system literally became another culture of the school. The e-mail conferences ranged from entertainment to those closer to courses. They became a place where the most serious and sophisticated discourse in the school took place, where students engaged in levels of debate that you rarely see anywhere."

Moretti was an early fan of multimedia; both junior and senior pupils at Dalton were building multimedia materials in the mid-Eighties. A recent CD-ROM which he developed with a colleague shows the power of the technology. The subject was the Rodney King case, the controversial trial about alleged police brutality in California. "It was one of the most important events in American racial history," says Moretti. "In future years, it will be consigned to a paragraph in history – a student will be required to know that the Rodney King case occurred in Los Angeles, and although people might have a discussion, the questions will be unrelated to the actual circumstances."

On the CD-ROM, Moretti has gathered together a video of the trial, the entire 20,000-word transcript of the trial, photographs, arrest papers plus other key documents, and 300 newspaper articles from the *Los Angeles Times* and the *Los Angeles Sentinel*. "Using the material we chose," he says, "you could come to almost any conclusion about the case." He has also added three tools. A search engine allows students to type in keywords to find any item on the CD-ROM. Then there is a worksheet in which selected items can be placed for analysis. A student might be asked to to take the first 10 seconds of the holiday video footage of the beating, break it down into three sections, and write a paragraph on each section; or to look at the evidence from the key witnesses and find the most telling evidence for the prosecution. Finally, there is a word processor for writing reports that can be linked back to the basic data. Moretti says: "This is the way a historian would work – you have a set of data, and you select some of it and elevate it into facts in your argument."

The Rodney King CD-ROM illustrates Moretti's theory that new technologies create unpredictability in two ways. First, they make a plethora of information available, in the way that no textbook can. Second, armed with powerful software for analysing real information, a student can arrive at any one of hundreds of conclusions, to which the teacher must respond. But there is no value, he says, in being let loose with infinite amounts of information, and the job of educators is to define the boundaries in which the children operate.

"I have no interest in a school where they spend all their time flopping around in cyberspace. That is not going to bring about an educational revolution. The nitty gritty is the counterbalance between tools and data, and structuring the motivational hook that mobilises the student's interest in using something. Sometimes the motivation is implicit – in a trial people are curious about innocence and guilt. In an archaeological simulation, anyone who begins becomes an archaeologist: 'You, sixth grade, have been asked to go to Greece and excavate this site; your job is to produce a site report for the Greek people. This is a very prestigious thing, and you have six weeks to do it.' In other instances, it is just in the nature of the questions you ask."

At Columbia Moretti is now working with a testbed of 100 schools in New York, with the aid of a $10 million grant from the Department of Education, hoping to demonstrate that things done at Dalton can be brought to most schools. Another project, the Earth Curriculum, has students working with information as it is collected by sensors that are in the natural environment. It is designed to cater for both the basic State curriculum and constructivist teaching methods. He says: "The tools allow teachers, depending on how adventurous they are, to engage students in a number of ways, ranging from an instructionally-driven style to something much more engaging and demanding.

"You can do one of two things in schools. You can take digital technologies, which in my opinion are radical – the most rudimentary alternative to the printing press since the printing press was invented – and you can use them within the constraints of older technologies, or you can push on the old constraints, which you have to do to discover the possibilities of the new. I am completely convinced that there will be radical new forms of education that will emerge if we have enough people who have the courage to begin to understand what kind of architecture and work environments the new technologies demand."

CHANGING RELATIONSHIPS

Will we see radical new forms of education emerge? Judging by the findings of one of the world's longest-running studies of the effects of technology in schools, the answer is yes – and the process will happen naturally. Apple Classrooms of Tomorrow (ACOT), a collaboration among schools, universities, research agencies and Apple Computer Inc., was initiated in the USA in 1985. ACOT began its work in seven classrooms that represented a cross-section of America's elementary and secondary schools. Its goal: to create environments in which technology was used as routinely as paper and books – and then observe the effects on teaching and learning.

After a decade, researchers had studied learning, assessment, teaching, teacher development, school design, the social aspects of education, and the use of new technologies in more than 100 classrooms. The results, published in *Teaching, Learning and Technology – A Report on 10 Years of ACOT Research* , provide a fascinating insight into the long-term effects of classroom technology, which it has not been possible to study on any scale in Britain.

ACOT research demonstrated improved academic performance, enhanced problem-solving ability and better attendance records. An interesting finding – because it is sometimes suggested that children's motivation may lessen as the novelty of computers and the Internet wears off – was that instead of becoming boring with use, technology was even more interesting to students when they began using it creatively and collaboratively. Over time, they tended to become independent learners and self-starters, knew their areas of expertise and shared that expertise spontaneously, and developed a positive attitude to the future.

As ACOT teachers became comfortable with the technology, they reported that they were enjoying their work more and feeling more successful. And they worked in a new way with their students – more as guides and mentors and less like lecturers. In fact, their personal efforts to make technology an integral part of their classrooms caused them to rethink their most basic beliefs about education. Barry Stebbins, science teacher at West High School, Columbus, Ohio, said: "ACOT has revitalised the teaching process tremendously. It has also been the catalyst for a transition from blackboards and textbooks to a method of instruction where students can explore, discover and construct their own knowledge." His colleague, maths teacher Paula Fistick, said: "As you work using the computer in the classroom, you start questioning everything you have done in the past, and wonder how you can adapt it to the computer. Then, you start questioning the whole concept of what you originally did." And an anonymous comment: "The experience has made me take risks. I have decided the worst that can happen is that I make mistakes and need to ask others for help."

Now, in its second decade, ACOT is collaborating with schools internationally to explore constructivism, with the emphasis on collaboration over the Internet.

TEACHERS AS LEARNERS

Already new teachers – 30,000 enter the profession in the UK every year – are reaping the benefits of technology in their own training. Student teachers, working in schools, keep in touch with college tutors via e-mail, and even use videoconferencing to relive their classroom triumphs and worst nightmares. BT's CampusTutor, a computer with videoconferencing and e-mail, allows class sessions either to be transmitted live to a tutor, or recorded for later review. Former teacher Linda Burdon, now BT's Teacher Training Manager, says: "If a student teacher is having problems managing a particular classroom activity, they can be filmed, then send the film back down the line to a tutor and discuss what else might have worked. What you don't want is your tutor sitting in your class, because the children act differently. When there is a stranger at the back, they are usually much better behaved."

To prepare themselves for the future, all teachers are going to have to be confident users of technology. The most successful training schemes help them to learn on the job, in the context of what they are trying to achieve in the classroom. That way, they are more likely to find sound reasons for wanting to continue, rather than using technology just because it is compulsory. Ian Gilchrist of BECTA ran the recent TRENDS project, a European initiative in which 2,400 teachers from seven countries were trained *in situ*. They learned how the Internet could be used as a classroom resource, by trying out ideas in their classes and then reporting back to other teachers and their tutors online.

"Teachers are ashamed to admit they don't know about technology," says Gilchrist. A common example is a very expensive machine that sits on the head teacher's desk, never used. "For people who have never been exposed to computers, I explain that it makes teaching easier. When I was a teacher, at parents' evenings, the parents looked at me, but the children made straight for the machines. I talk about The Sage on the Stage – the traditional teacher at the front of the class lecturing – and The Guide on the Side, the computer there as an active, engaging tool for learning."

The prototype of the National Grid For Learning provided an incentive for teachers to go online; it was launched in January 1998 as The Virtual Teacher Centre, 'a place for teachers to go for inspiration and help in raising standards'. And one of the best incentives of all is to give teachers their own computers. The BECTA Portables For Teachers project, launched in 1996, gave 1,150 teachers their own multimedia laptop computers – 98 per cent used them successfully in and outside the classroom.

Rather than 'sheep dipping' all teachers – immersing them all in standard ICT training, software can make the process more personal. BT has come up with a program designed to help individual teachers assess exactly what technology skills they need. The ASSESS software takes primary and secondary staff through a set of questions about their job, then suggests which tools could be useful and how to find training. BT's Linda Burdon says: "A teacher may not be able to build a database, but that may not be necessary for everyone. Up till now, nobody has been looking at what people need to teach their particular subject."

But there are other skills that will have to be mastered. How, for example, do you assess a child who is writing a story with the aid of a word processor? With pen and paper, a pupil produces the final report and it is marked. Switch to the computer, however, and a draft copy could be produced first, and the structure and ideas discussed with the teacher. In the computer-assisted scenario, both student and teacher go through new intellectual processes. How do you assess collaborative work, or measure thinking skills? And if children are taking more of an active part in directing their own learning, how much will the process of learning count as against what has been learned? Many challenges lie ahead.

SCHOOL OF THE FUTURE?

For decades there have been brave attempts to gaze into the crystal ball at the School of the Future. Predicting the future is never easy; but today, there are more options than ever before. The 'connected' school is no longer constrained by its own walls – it can use distant teachers, resources, and even work remotely with far-away pupils.

Some of the groundwork for change is being laid in a project which will explore new patterns of schooling. Run jointly by the Funding Agency for Schools and the University of Lincolnshire and Humberside, the project aims to find a constructive alternative to building or extending schools to cope with the pressure of rising numbers of pupils. In London alone, it is estimated that up to 20,000 extra secondary places will be required by the year 2003. Yet currently, schools are used for only 13 per cent of the possible total time available. The premise is that by altering the school year, and using technology to support some independent learning, it should be possible to accommodate more pupils in the same space, and enhance learning opportunities by using money that would otherwise have been spent on building.

Still in the early stages, the project is to be piloted in three schools –

two in Bromley, Kent, and one in Barnet, north London. Pupils will be divided into different tracks, with each track following a different rota of holidays, teaching days, and self-managed learning days. At no time will all the pupils be in school at once, and the only common holiday will be the Christmas break.

Professor Brent Davies, director of the International Educational Leadership Centre at the University of Lincolnshire and Humberside, says: "If you have 180 kids in a school, in three tracks of 60, and you were to increase it to four tracks, making a total of 240 pupils, normally the cost of doing that would be about £1700 per place per year. We are suggesting we can accommodate those extra children in the school by getting them to come in at different times. The money we save on the capital cost should be spent on technology to enhance the learning day. None of the schools are interested simply in buying more equipment or getting more kids in. What they want to do is move the pattern of their learning so that it is more independent, student-focused or student-led learning.

"Normally teachers teach a 38-week year. Suppose we split the year into five eight-week terms in which seven were taught and one week was independent learning. Each child from the age of 11 would do one week of independent learning with the aid of structured self-learning materials. As we progress up the school, that proportion might be increased – we are looking at whether this is feasible. The teacher would be a facilitator of the learning package, but when the kids do technology-based stuff there wouldn't necessarily be a teacher there. In our cost profile, there would be half an advisory teacher or a technician. We have been looking at research into learning gains in America, where tracking is huge – 3 million children in about 3,000 schools are doing it."

He envisages that in future, children could do their independent learning either in a school technology centre or at home. "I don't envisage that by 2005 every kid will go to school five days a week. We have got to switch the emphasis from teaching them in buildings to them learning. I think things will change significantly. Most of the government emphasis now is on trying to get people to get hold of basic numeracy and literacy. But as you move up the school and you want more specialism, that's when it becomes more expensive in terms of smaller classes and more specialised equipment. Technology will fill that gap. So what you might get with schooling is very much the core, where the State gets you functional literacy and technology skills, and as you go up and take more diverse subjects, a lot of those will be technology-based. I don't think the whole country will change, but some innovative schools will. It will be fragmented, and there will be different patterns everywhere."

RE-THINKING THE SCHOOL

ICL's Chris Yapp believes that the whole educational system is ripe for change. He says: "The challenge isn't connecting every child to the Internet, but re-engineering education to support lifelong learning. Throwing IT at problems makes things worse if you don't understand what the problem is. You have to look at the organisation, its goals, and roles, and then apply technology to it – the technology does not automatically determine what you do.

"The three 'R's – the definition of an educated adult – was defined during the the Industrial Revolution. You have 50 per cent of the population working with information, but the school system is still modelled on the Industrial Revolution. If you now stand back and look at what skills you need to survive, the first question is: 'What is the purpose of education and training?'. Most people's goals are personal growth, social cohesion, and economic performance."

He draws comparisons with the manufacturing and retail industries, which have re-designed the way they operate. "They have moved from being production-led to being customer-led. Education is the last model of Fordism – you put children on a conveyor belt at the age of four and let them fall off at different stages. From a quality viewpoint, they fall off at the point at which they fail. But you can choose your car, so why can't you have millions of national curriculums? Why not have a curriculum that meets the needs of each child?"

Yapp believes that, like companies in other market sectors, schools will have to re-think the way they organise themselves. "In education, organisational change means asking : 'What is a school, and what is a teacher?' In the medical world, you have specialists – consultants, doctors, nurses, paraprofessionals. But a teacher is a guard, nanny, subject expert and administrator. A teacher's job is crazy.

"Smaller is now beautiful. We live in smaller communities, there are smaller units of production, even armies are getting smaller. But against that trend, schools, colleges and universities are getting bigger and bigger."

His vision is an educational system that "develops a generation of self-managed learners competent in the old and new literacies". He says: "You have to focus on self-managed learning, because you can't be taught everything you need to know. There are skills issues: what A levels do you do in order to become competent in drawing, software, hardware, design, video, film, animation, music and multimedia authoring? There will be a blurring of artistic, technical, scientific and personal skills. We are setting up arts and science colleges, but we need a blend of those skills. Maybe the secondary school of the future will have 200 pupils – the size of the primary – but every child will go to more than one school. Language, technology, all networked together. Schools, such as laboratory schools, will have a duty to share their resources with others. They won't be in competition – additional resources and spare capacity will be shared."

He believes that there is an opportunity to revitalise an education system which has long had problems: "The first report on under-achievement in British education was in 1854 from Prince Albert. The first quantitative study of our under-achievement in maths compared to

Germany was in 1918. So the idea that we had this perfect education system until the 1960s is not the case.

"Multimedia education in the UK is the largest single software market for technology in the next century. Learning is the largest industry. We can create new learning industries in the UK and capitalise on the value of the English language, which has to be our major asset, in order to fund education. We want an individual curriculum to international standards, not a national curriculum. It is competitiveness, but with social inclusion. That is the only way in which I think you can deliver lifelong learning for all.

"You can start to ask: 'What kind of society do we want to build?' rather than: 'How will society look?'. We are at a point where there is a certain amount of freedom to intervene. As we move from an industrial to a knowledge economy, we have the freedom to experiment and do things differently for inclusiveness. In a few years' time, the window may have closed."

⑥ Home-Schoolers

COMPUTERS are a valuable help in schools, but for parents who have chosen the alternative way of educating their children – at home – they can be a godsend. Sue Hutchin, of Bethersden, Kent, who is teaching eight-year-old Scarlett and 13-year-old Alex at home, says: "If I had no computer, my job would be much more difficult."

▲　　▲　　▲

When Alex was six, Sue read an article about home schooling, which she hadn't realised was possible. After doing some research and coming across Education Otherwise, a home-schooling support group, she took her son out of school. She and her husband Mark, an osteopath, who live and work in a rambling cottage down a quiet Kentish lane, use their computer as "a library, a games room and a social focus". They bought the PC because they felt they might be missing out on the technological back-up in schools. Sue admits she was doubtful about the machine at first, but is now pleasantly surprised at its value. "The software titles that we use are good tools, full of real information in an interesting format."

Sue's farmhouse kitchen-table tuition doesn't work to an overall plan or curriculum, but picks up on the children's enthusiasm to learn. Scarlett, say her parents, taught herself to read: her first word was 'foot' because she liked the shape of it on a footpath sign. She now has a passion for reading – her current favourites are *A Midsummer Night's Dream* and *Under Milk Wood* – and she writes stories with the aid of a children's word processor, although when she started to write, her spelling was so phonetic that the spellchecker couldn't recognise any words. She now produces fluent prose for family projects, and her spelling has caught up.

Scarlett says: "The computer doesn't make me write better, but it makes me enjoy writing better." Sue says: "I tried teaching her reading and writing and failed completely – it was a miserable waste of time in which she made no progress and I got angry. She still won't do joined-up handwriting – she prefers the word-processor – but I won't force her. She is so interested in drawing that I can't believe she will always be content to have dreadful handwriting."

Scarlett is keen on archaeology – when she was seven she gave her family a guided tour of the British Museum's Egyptian Rooms based on the knowledge she had picked up from a CD-ROM on ancient lands. And when she wants to find out about nature, she spends some time with a nature CD-ROM, then goes to help Mum dig the garden. "We have loads of books too," says her mother. The computer isn't the only resource, but – an important factor for home schoolers working on shoestring budgets – it is compact and cheaper than print. "Our £30 paper atlas hasn't got 1 per cent of the information in an atlas on CD-ROM."

Alex loves maths, and the 13-year-old is now ready to take his GCSE. In return for a small exam fee, he will sit this in a local grammar school, surrounded by 400 16-year-old girls. His mother says he is confident: "For Alex, the exercise is not about getting a 'C'." Sue prepared Alex with the aid of one book from the local bookshop, which they worked through together. She couldn't find any software that was appropriate: "I tried out one package on approval, but it was so tedious that nobody would have used it, and it couldn't answer back when we were stuck."

Alex did, however, use the computer to make his GCSE coursework look professional, laboriously constructing mathematical symbols using drawing software. (Sue: "I thought no-one handed in pen-and-ink work these days.") When his work was assessed as a favour by a teacher friend, it was placed in the top A* category. Beyond the exam, he may consider taking a vocational qualification in computer programming – another passion – at a local open learning college.

Sue shuns children's 'edutainment' software. "I have looked at a lot of the kind where you have to add up four and four to get to kill the Gruzzles. I'm not very keen on disguising things to make them fun. Maths is exciting for Alex, because he loves solving the problems, and Scarlett wanted to do arithmetic so she could add up her pocket money. We are in the real world here, not the Land of the Gruzzles."

The family have begun to explore the Internet, but feel they need to hone their searching skills before it becomes a worthwhile, affordable resource. As Sue says: "There is so much to learn, and we have no time to waste."

BOOM AT HOME

Homeschooling is booming: cautious estimates suggest that 10,000 families in Britain now educate their children at home, and that 100 families a month are taking their children out of school. The real figures are probably much higher, because, although home schooling is perfectly legal, some local authorities frown upon on it and make life difficult for home educators. Many families simply choose to remain anonymous. The Education Act of 1944, re-inforced by the Act of 1996, says that parents must provide an education that is appropriate to a child's age, aptitude and special needs, at school or otherwise. Parents choose the 'otherwise' option for many reasons, from religious beliefs through to disillusionment with the school system.

Home-schoolers take a variety of approaches to educating their children; some work to a formal curriculum and age targets, others simply pick up on their children's enthusiasms as they emerge, arguing that youngsters learn more receptively when they really want to know about something. Some are spurred on by the success of the home schooling movement in the USA, where over 600,000 families homeschool, an estimated 80 per cent of them because of religious beliefs. Many are inspired by the work of US educators such as the late John Holt, who wrote widely about how children could be nurtured to drive their own learning, and who came to believe that homeschooling was the way to change an education system that was failing children.

Thanks largely to US organisations, the Internet is packed with information for homeschoolers. A visit to a major site such as The HomeSchooling Information Library or Lytingale's HomeSchooling and Educational Resources yields a treasure trove of advice and resources. Parents can swap or sell curriculums or materials, seek advice, and find links to educational resources and as well as worldwide projects that children can share via the Internet. Although many international projects are aimed primarily at schools, there are plenty of opportunities for home-based learners to join in the fun. Internet clubs such as Kids' Space bring together e-pals, and provide a Web showcase for children's drawings, stories and music. At the site run by Childnet, the UK charity set up to encourage children to get involved in the Internet, there are projects that range from following a historic schooner as she sails round the Pacific through to conducting lifestyle surveys. Even though much of the educational material is aimed at the North American market, it can be a boon to British homeschoolers, who are often less constrained by a curriculum than schools. Some parents use the Net to keep one step ahead of their children, others to follow up quickly on children's enthusiasms.

Malcolm Muckle set up the Web site for Education Otherwise, the UK homeschooling self-help group, in 1996. He says: "Education

Otherwise is very much a DIY organisation – people tend to do their own thing as a family, and styles of learning are very much evolving. More and more people are finding our Web site, including Americans who are coming to Europe and want to know what the situation is here. In the USA, homeschooling is growing at 15-17 per cent per year – so much so that in some states, people are nervous that the government might say: 'Hang on a moment, let's have a closer look at this.' It is almost a victim of its own success."

He says that computers can be a big help, although home-educators, many of them single-parents, always yearn for bigger machines and smaller phone bills. He believes the greatest value of the Internet is for making contact between people: finding mutual support networks, sharing learning between families with similar interests, and helping people who run into problems or trouble with local authorities, whose attitudes vary widely. In some areas, particularly deprived districts, homeschoolers have a fruitful relationship with the authorities, while in others, they find themselves having to move to escape intolerant inspectors and social services departments. The Internet proved a valuable tool to one woman who was having a long-runnning dispute with an inspector. After she threatened to publish the whole correspondence from the saga on the Web – 50 letters back and forth – an amicable agreement was reached.

Using the Internet is only one of many ways homeschoolers socialise, although Muckle believes it may play a more important role now that personal software agents are beginning to make an appearance on the Internet. He says: "You can have your own little bit of computer software sitting somewhere. It will keep an eye open for what it knows you are particularly interested in – it tunes into your preferences, and when you say: 'I like this but not that', it tries to do better on its next search. Now agents are also being designed so that when one meets another, they exchange information about their interests."

FLEXISCHOOLING

A few children are also involved in flexischooling – mixing and matching home-based and formal education. As Alex Hutchin plans to do in Kent, some children take a course with a local open learning college, learning either at the college or at a distance, and many course materials are being made available on the Internet. Other families come to an agreement whereby a child registers at a state school but shows up for only certain subjects, although there are few success stories, as schools find it difficult to make the arrangement work and often feel it is disruptive for full-time pupils. And anyway, as they get older, home-schooled children often tend to go back into formal education. Malcolm Muckle says: "Beyond the age of 12 or 13 there is quite a steep drop off. Parents may not be able to survive on low incomes, especially if more children come along. They may want children to have formal qualifications that they can wave at universities, or maybe the children themselves feel they are missing out on something or simply don't want to be different any more."

Homeschooling parent John Paddon dreams for the day when he can flexischool his two sons. "What a beautiful world," he says. "My own feeling is that homeschooling is the norm, and school should be the last-ditch effort. If there was something that was a combination of the two – all the expertise and the resources of the people who are dedicated to teaching, together with the home-nurtured, home-grown, one-to-one-attention, this country would be unstoppable." His vision is that schools could be divided into centres of expertise that children could learn to tap into, just as they will have to do in their adult lives. John can claim to have more of an interest than most – he has just trained to be a teacher.

"I didn't really set out to do it," he says. "But I thought I needed some kind of paper qualification to become a consultant in business." While his wife Jenny worked as a registrar during the day, he stayed at home in Bolton with sons Laurence, 7, Alex, 8, and 10-year-old Liam, and he went out to study in the evenings.

The boys have always been educated at home. John says: "At the moment I have pulled back from formal teaching and making them do things and even from having a set pattern. We are leaving it for them to develop, and from time to time we sit down and run through different bits and pieces out of our own heads, or anything we have picked up ourselves. They use us as a resource in their learning."

All the boys have learned to touch-type on the family computer: Alex began before he could read or write, exactly as Lawrence has decided to do now. John says: "Liam already has a great deal of enthusiasm for reading and writing, and has been using the computer to write stories for a long time. I tried telling him he had a schedule to write a book – one way of being more liberal and yet getting him to work to some kind of deadline – but it didn't go down well. When I pulled back he came into it again. It is worth building his skills, because writing is an ideal livelihood for someone who is home-educated and who may not go for qualifications."

Jenny's decision to link the family to the Internet as a major source of information has had surprising results. The Net failed to prove a draw for the boys, who never use it, but their father developed a real interest. Used to tinkering with computers to make the family's budget stretch further, he linked to computing conferences on the Internet, discovered that he really knew quite a lot about the subject, and has opted to make a living from it. He has been offered a job training staff at a local computer company. He says: "I force myself to sit on the Internet for an hour on weekend mornings, when the phone rate is cheapest and before the Americans start using the Internet and slowing it down. I just dredge for information – at the moment I am looking for software for disabled learners."

He says the household doesn't own any educational software: "I don't know what's out there, and it all seems to be a lot of hype. It amounts to very little when you get hold of it – they don't seem to know how to use the technology to really maximise the potential." Most family software, including three encyclopedias on CD-ROM, comes free with computer magazines.

John sums up the family learning strategy: "It's very loose, I'm afraid. I say 'afraid' because I am so used to people saying: 'You can't do that unless you are a professor.' But if you look, particularly at Laurence, who has been breast-fed, and allowed to decide when he moves on to another stage of learning, his development has been amazing. He seems to be so enthusiastic about what he does – he gets an idea, develops it and works through a scheme. Although it is not academic, you can see how in future he will be able to learn or develop any field of interest that he has. The system tries to knock the self-confidence out of people and then tries to put it back in afterwards. I have tried to teach people who have come out of school, but you can't seem to get any rapport with them at all, even on a one-to-one basis, which is the way I like to work with most people – eye-to-eye. To them it was 'them and us'."

IN PURSUIT OF KNOWLEDGE

Other people share the view that school can be a crushing experience. In 1991, US teacher John Gatto celebrated being named New York State Teacher of the Year by penning an essay, *The Six-Lesson Schoolteacher* that slammed established methods of teaching. It culminated in the intriguing estimate that it takes only 50 hours of contact to transmit basic literacy and maths skills well enough for children to be self-teachers from then onwards.

Roland Meighan is a professor at Nottingham University and founder of Education Now, which campaigns for more flexible and personalised education, whether in school or at home. He says: "I think John Gatto was being pessimistic with that figure. A number of home educators who have kept an eye on this have said the same thing – it takes 30 hours. Some say it is 30 hours in one splurge – I can think of one person who said her youngster was slow in learning to read, and then suddenly said: 'I am ready to learn now'. He learned in a fortnight – that was logged as 30 hours. That just happened at the time the child had a burning drive to do it.

"It really does blow apart the cause of schools. John Holt used to say that after years and years of schooling, children are less intelligent than when they started and I can see his point, because an awful lot of their time has been wasted. The problem is that increasingly in schools we have set up hostile learning conditions, and learning to read and so on becomes a problem because people's motivation is under pressure and they are afraid of making mistakes. George Bernard Shaw said: 'What we want to see is the child in pursuit of knowledge, not knowledge in pursuit of the child.' It gets over the whole business of hunting children – and teachers – down."

"Home-based education should be part of a mosaic that also includes flexitime schooling and institutions. We should open our institutions up so they are flexible places of learning, not day prisons."

He says that technology, although not an essential part of flexible education, can be an "extraordinarily good tool", and that new technology is showing up the inefficiency of schools. "We now have CD-ROMs which will guarantee to get you O-level maths in a quarter of the time of a taught course. Work at home with an interactive CD-ROM and you save time as well as the pain of being exposed in class as being a bit slow. A chap I know said that as a geography teacher he used to teach plate tectonics – earth movements and volcanoes – and it took him six one-hour lessons. He looked at his son's CD-ROM, and the subject took half an hour. He said: 'In that half-hour my son said it covered everything I covered in six hours only better, because it was visual and had moving diagrams. And you can go back and play it again to check something. You couldn't go back over my lessons.'"

Meighan's predictions: "Technology will blow our concept of the day prison out of the water in the end, simply by the revolt of parents who are seeing more and more of this kind of thing and saying: 'What are we wasting our time for?' The education system has to move into much more flexible patterns, and recognise realities such as the fact that the academic curriculum is dying because the whole market for the clerk and super-clerk is drying up. The growth areas in the economy are the media, leisure and personal services. The clerk – whether it is banking or civil service or even the medical profession – is dying. We now even have CD-ROMs that can beat the doctor to the diagnosis every time."

❼ Difficulties and Disabilities

MARTIN sits at the computer screen and displays his story: it is about family, football and going to the pub. If anyone feigns shock about the pub, the teenager laughs uproariously. Martin has cerebral palsy; he can hardly use his voice, and has little control of his limbs. But he is a successful communicator, being the proud owner of a 'good yes' – a strong nod of his head to signify agreement. This is the basis for all his face-to-face dealings with people, and now it is helping him use computers to reach a wider audience. Martin attends Meldreth Manor School in Hertfordshire, a residential school run by the cerebral palsy charity Scope. It is expert in helping youngsters find a way to express themselves, even though their communication may consist of no more than a blink or a movement of the tongue. Where appropriate, technology is called upon to help.

▲   ▲   ▲

One successful development has been to get pupils on to the Internet. When headmaster David Banes announced this plan at a computer show, he didn't get much support. "People told me it wasn't worth it," he says, "But we are rather obstinate here. The Internet is a great leveller – you can make friends without having to focus on your disabilities."

Thanks to this stubbornness, a delighted bunch of kids are now using the Net to send news to their families, make friends around the world, and check the latest football results. This is not a miracle brought about by modern technology, but the result of a lot of hard work by pupils and teachers. For Martin and his school friends, the journey to reach the superhighway can be a long one.

Martin arrived at Meldreth in 1994, at the age of 15. He may have brought his 'good yes' to answer questions with, but it was of limited use, because he had no way of indicating what the questions should be about. His first year was spent mastering Rebus, a pictorial language that helps people who have difficulty with speech, writing or words. Martin's personalised Rebus communication board, a piece of card containing the symbols he uses most, accompanies him everywhere. By looking at a section of the board, he assists people to home in on the right group of symbols, then he nods in agreement when the exact one he wants is chosen. It is a simple but remarkably effective system, and now Martin is also using an adapted version on a computer.

The entire collection of 3,500 Rebus symbols lives on a PC, courtesy of software called Working With Symbols. Another program, called Switch Clicker, displays a selection of these in a screen-based grid. The squares in the grid are automatically highlighted one after another. The trick is to choose a symbol by freezing the highlight on a particular square. For most at Meldreth Manor, using a computer mouse is out of the question, which means they are treated to much more fascinating gizmos. A range of devices, collectively labelled switches, allows each child to use his or her own way of saying 'yes' to control the computer. Some switches are driven by raising an eyebrow, some by blinking, and Martin's is strapped to his chest, so that when he nods, his chin clicks the switch, and a choice is made on the screen.

With the help of Wendy, his language therapist, Martin can construct a story, see it printed in symbols and words, and thanks to voice synthesis software, he can listen to it too. Once a child has got this far, a teacher can then use Working With Symbols to turn the story into straight text, pour it into an e-mail, and send it around the world. As Martin finishes his story, two classmates work with their headmaster on the Internet. They listen to their new e-mail – it is converted and read out – and visit some favourite Web sites (reggae music and yet more football). The school has its own Web pages, which are linked to the Scope site, but as the headmaster says: "They would much rather visit the Bob Marley home page than read about wheelchairs."

"Who is the worst person in the school at using the Internet?" he asks. "You," replies one of his pupils. Martin and his friends understand how the Internet works, thanks to some down-to-earth teaching which could usefully be adopted elsewhere. ("Let's link these two PCs here together with this wire so we can send messages between them. Now, how far could a wire stretch between computers? All the way around the world if we used the phone line as a wire.")

But surfing the Web still calls for a helper to interpret what's happening, because of a couple of technical drawbacks. First, says headmaster Banes, there is no easy way to extract text from a Web page, and so the content can't be converted to Rebus and read out. And as yet, there is no software that highlights all the 'hotspots' on a page in turn, so that someone using a switch can make a selection. "As soon as we think we have got somewhere with the software," says David Banes, "a new browser comes along and we have to start all over again. But at least it ensures that Web use is a social event."

The school has invested in standard-issue PCs: although hardware could be adapted, say, to fit flat on to a wheelchair, the idea is to equip the children to use any machine. But the most important idea, says Banes, is Never Trust The Computer. "We teach the children not to be overly dependent on technology. You always need low-tech to support the high-tech in case the computer breaks down." His next plan is to explore virtual reality, and he is very excited by its potential. "Some people say that these kids shouldn't experience it, because it would be too confusing," he says. "But it allows them to experience things which are otherwise out of the question – whether it is skiing down a mountain, or moving through a fantasy world using their wheelchair as a spacecraft. It is a new kind of learning environment."

The Internet has been instructive in all kinds of ways. "Some friends in California told the kids about helper dogs," says Banes. "If you drop things, the dog picks them up for you, and it barks when you move your wheelchair. Now all the kids here want one. That shows that they are aspirational. They see things that are different for someone somewhere else, and say: 'I want some of that.'"

David Banes explains the philosophy behind Martin's education: "Martin's disability is global – it impacts all his interactions with his environment – and his physical disability is non-remediable, in that he will never walk or have control over his own body. But what we can do is alleviate some of the effects by changing the environment rather than changing Martin." Some people face barriers to learning because of specific difficulties; others, such as Martin, face a whole range of challenges which impact on every area of their lives. There is a now a wealth of technology that can play a part in enhancing their lives and giving them more access to the world.

DO YOU WANT THE SCREEN?

At Knowetop Primary School in Motherwell, Scotland, Monica McGeever is support teacher for children with visual impairments. She teaches Braille, but also ensures that her young charges, three of whom are blind, have access to the mainstream curriculum, which increasingly involves using computers. Despite many years of experience, it was only when Monica visited a parent, who is also blind, that it really struck home how the computer experience must be for the children. "She is very knowledgeable about technology, and I went to see her computer system," says Monica. "It was only after she had fired the machine up and started work that she said: 'Do you want the screen on?'"

Thanks to a £1,000 award from computer services company EDS, Monica is now using a Braille 'n' Speak computer, a tiny word-processing machine which has a Braille keyboard but no screen. As children type, the machine reads their work back to them, or they can store the text and listen later. The machine can also be linked to an embossing machine that produces hard copies in Braille, or hooked up to a PC and printed for teachers and friends. The Braille 'n' Speak is now being used to prepare two girls for their move to secondary school, and the computer whizz-kid parent is helping them get some practice. Monica says: "The idea is that they will be able to take notes as they move from class to class. A normal Brailler is very heavy and not portable, but the new machine is very small – 15cm by 10cm. They can save the notes, and hear them read back at night at home."

She says that although Braille serves as the main method of communication for the girls, they also use a mainstream QWERTY keyboard, and are taught to touch-type. At the moment the keyboard is attached to a machine called a Languagemaster, a talking dictionary and thesaurus. The purchase of a screen-reader – software that reads out not just typed documents, but absolutely everything that is happening on a screen – will enable the youngsters to use a standard computer, and take them one step further towards a future career.

Monica says technology can also help in other ways. "When I was a schoolgirl, the kind of work we were asked to do was so different. Now there are so many assignments and projects that are based on research, even at primary school. We start homework projects in primary 4 – that's quite young – and primary 5 is doing a huge six-week project on different methods of transport. For children with visual impairments that can be so difficult. They can't move around like other children – their parents are often more protective – and even if they make it to the library, the print is sometimes too small to read. If you have the CD-ROM encyclopedias and the Internet at home, much more information becomes accessible."

HELP FOR DYSLEXICS

Kate Bennett is special needs co-ordinator at Ramridge Infants School, in Luton, Bedfordshire. She says: "As soon as a teacher alerts me that a child is not getting on – say word matching or copying, the general pre- and early reading activities – I try to assess whether it is going to be an ongoing school difficulty or whether the child is, say, lacking in confidence or not used to books and words. I decide how much extra help they need."

She is now exploring the use of software to help identify learning difficulties at any early stage. The children play games that test their visual and auditory skills. Kate says: "It records the child's attempts – you see how they got it right and wrong and how long they took. As a teacher, I find it fascinating to watch the tests. For example, there is a rabbits game – the rabbits visit holes, and you have to remember which holes the rabbit last went down, in which order. One child chose the same holes every time. With the older children, if they feel they are not getting it right they just rush through the rest of the test. It is actually a good reflection on their learning styles. Another game displays a hieroglyphic then asks the child to identify it from a group. It is like presenting a child with the alphabet for the first time – we see it from the child's point of view."

Other tests include a rhyming game – Kate says there is a lot of evidence that children who can't hear rhymes are likely to have difficulty with reading and or spelling – and a game that tests hearing, as some degree of hearing loss is very common in young children. She says that as well as identifying weaknesses, the games also pick out their strengths. "We have a child who we were fairly certain was dyslexic because there is a family history of it. His parents both said: 'Oh dear, another one – just like his brother'. But when I did the tests with him, he came out well on all of them. We are now going to meet the parents again and say it seems to us that he has got low expectations of himself. I can show them how well he has done – print out the details of the tests. The software also shows how an average child would score in each area."

One of the problems with dyslexia, says Kate, is that educational psychologists are reluctant to diagnose a child as dyslexic before the age of eight, because children grow out of a lot of the symptoms, such as reversing letters or numbers. "I don't think we should be labelling children as dyslexic very early. But what is good about these games is that we can pick up children who may have some signs and work into their programme of work some remedial measures that would be relevant to a child with dyslexia."

She says: "I would love to be able to do this all day, but I am teaching as well. I spend dinner times doing the tests – but on wet days, all the children are inside so you can't hear properly, and can't do it."

The British Dyslexia Association estimates that around four per cent of the population shows some signs of dyslexia, specific difficulties with memory, organisation and processing language. It can affect the learning of reading, writing, spelling, number work and music. Ciaran Holland of Interactive Services markets software for diagnosing adult dyslexics which is currently on trial at 15 universities. In privacy, students take an initial set of exercises to find out whether it is worth going on to the second stage – a full-blown computer-based dyslexia test that produces a 16-page analysis. He says: "Around 60 per cent of people with dyslexia have made it through school and on to college without being diagnosed. If they are diagnosed at college, they are entitled to half an hour extra in which to do each exam, and a government grant of £3,000-4,000." Some people find that technology can help them develop strategies for coping with dyslexia. Dictating to a computer, rather than writing or typing can be a boon, and by slowing their speech down so that the computer can keep pace, some dyslexics have found they have been more able to recognise the words on the screen. Computers also allow scope for altering fonts and colours, which may often help.

TALKING IN SIGNS

Remarkable new technologies continue to be developed. Sister Mary of the Internet, for example, is an American project to develop a computer system that will recognise American Sign Language for the Deaf. The user who is signing wears special 'datagloves', which are fitted with sensors that detect the position and movement of the fingers and wrists. The gloves are connected to a computer, and as the user signs, the Sister Mary system picks up and interprets the gestures. At the moment, Sister Mary can record and play back the gestures and translate from English into sign language. The next target is translating signed input into English. This kind of system could act as an intermediary in all sorts of conversations, and the project team at the Applied Science and Engineering Laboratories in Delaware are also working on how to change Sister Mary's expression in tune with what she is saying. Other researchers are looking at how to use datagloves to communicate with deaf-blind people. The idea is to send signals from a computer that produce pressure on the fingertips of the glove, like another person using the manual alphabet.

But in other cases, very simple ideas and long-in-the-tooth technology can work wonders. In 1997, Deaf@x Trust, a charity for the deaf, teamed up with BT and BECTA in a simple scheme to provide deaf children with 'fax buddies'. The idea was to encourage children between the ages of 7 and 14 to improve their reading and writing by corresponding by fax with adults in BT and BECTA. The scheme was low-cost, with some schools managing to persuade companies to donate an old machine that would otherwise have ended up on the scrap heap. The adults were given guidelines on how to converse with deaf children, many of whom use British Sign Language as their first language and find it difficult to express themselves in English. They have problems dealing with long words and sentences, and many do not understand how a two-way conversation works. Evaluation of the project showed that as the children built a rapport with their buddies, they were spurred on to develop their literacy skills, explore new grammar and syntax, and communicate more openly. A teacher said of one girl: "It was interesting to see her using the fax to tell her buddies about the time she had been naughty in school and explaining the punishment she had received. It almost seemed like a way for her to get something out of her system, which was difficult for her to communicate in other ways." Deaf@x also encourages deaf people of all ages to find e-pals via its Web site, and they sometimes find themselves helping a hearing person from abroad to learn English as a second language.

DISABLED LEAD THE WAY

Bill Fine is a consultant at the Computability Centre, a charity aimed at making computing more accessible for everyone. Although some of his work is directed at helping people with profound disabilities, he believes fervently that many able-bodied people are also suffering because they can't adjust to what is considered to be the normal way of using a computer. He says: "Anybody who finds the ordinary ways of working a computer unsatisfactory – difficult, painful or tiring – can choose from 200 other techniques. They don't have to give up. But people buy these immensely powerful machines, and then everybody gets the same input device. Left-handed people have to work with a right-handed keyboard, and people have to be signed off work because their hand hurts when they use a mouse, but nobody has told them they don't have to. It's like pedalling a Ferrari – and anyone who isn't strong enough to pedal is labelled 'disabled'."

Fine says that although some of the technology is "sexy and wonderful" ("You can have a little reflective spot on your forehead or your glasses, and by moving your head you can both type and use a mouse") – he helps more people with solutions that don't cost a thing. "We run a workshop called low-cost solutions in which we don't mention anything that costs more than £100 to buy. Much of it is free because it uses existing facilities on systems, such as the accessibility features built into the Windows 95 software on PCs."

He believes that disabled people are heading the drive to find better ways to use computers. "They are saying: 'I can't put up with this – I need something else'. I show disabled people how to type 'Yours sincerely' with two keystrokes. Then I go and tell other people, and they say: 'Why am I still typing out the whole words – this isn't about disability, is it?' He says that the needs of the disabled drove the development of voice-recognition systems, now a cheap and commonplace commodity provided free with many computers. But he warns: "The developments are so remarkable that there is a danger that in the next couple of years we will float from the assumption that everyone should use a keyboard and mouse to the assumption that everybody should use voice. That will be equally destructive.

"We are talking about people's lives here. I had a former education minister here and he said: 'Gosh, some of this technology must make a lot of difference to children'. I said: 'Yes, but tell me what would happen to the education budget if it were deemed to be the right of every child to communicate as well as they can be allowed to?' We are not even remotely close to giving children that right. Some children with articulate parents in imaginative educational authorities with decent special needs budgets will do OK. Others will get absolutely nothing."

PUSHING THE LIMITS

Back at Meldreth Manor, David Banes keeps pushing on the limits of what can be done with technology. He is now building on the children's mastery of switches to help them control their own wheelchairs, first with the aid of a special track, a copper strip that has been laid in and around the school. There is a sensor on the wheelchair so that when a student presses any switch and the sensor finds the track, it moves the chair along. Some 'smart chairs' have sensors that can detect and avoid walls and furniture. David Banes says: "Of course, if the technology breaks down, we still have to give them a way to tell somebody who's pushing them how to help. But the track is the first stage of independent mobility. You now have control to start and stop yourself, take yourself to where you want to be. We are looking at the whole area of aspirations – is there a link between independent mobility and having high expectations of what else you can do in your life?"

One of his most fascinating schemes is his work with a device called a Soundbeam, which conjures music out of thin air. Perfected by musician David Jackson, the Soundbeam system uses an ultrasonic beam to detect people moving in a room, and translates their movements into sounds and tones via a musical keyboard and synthesiser. Soundbeams can be programmed to mix and match everything from excerpts of Chopin sonatas to space-movie sound effects. David Jackson makes albums of Soundbeam music, but he also takes the technology out to schools to help students find a unique and wonderful way of expressing themselves.

For children with very restricted movement, there are techniques that can make even the simplest gesture expressive, and the technology allows instruments to be tailor-made to suit the interests and abilities of each child. Jackson worked with a boy who was only interested in trampolining – he couldn't do it, but made trampolining gestures with his upper body and arms. So Jackson used the Soundbeam to make an instrument that produced various trampolining noises when the boy moved. It helped the youngster develop some control over his movements and to become more expressive.

At Meldreth, the equipment is being used not just to unlock a talent to make a noise, but also to let the children see what it is like to express themselves to a public audience. Putting on a series of Soundbeam concerts has raised their self-esteem, and has had them working hard to reach performance level. David Banes, headmaster at Meldreth Manor, says: "We have spent a long time working on formal communication skills, but helping the kids to express emotions has been harder. The Soundbeam work is about releasing creativity and expression. Martin was on Radio 1, making Soundbeam music, and that was the high point for him – he decided it was to be Hollywood next, and that his next date should be with the Spice Girls."

Banes is also starting out on a choreography project that will give children with very limited control over their own bodies, a language and vocabulary by which they can control able-bodied dancers. "They are all symbols users, so the challenge is to create symbols that represent things a body can do, that the children can string together as choreography for a dancer. If you have a piece of music that makes you feel sad, how do you string together a sequence of movements to move someone else's body to repeat that sadness and present it in another way?

"Are we pushing them to hard? We don't know – but at the moment they are enjoying it. We see all these things as 3-4 year projects, and ultimately we will bring the Soundbeam and the dance together. Music will be composed, you will turn that into dance movement through symbols, but then those dances will be performed in front of the Soundbeam, and create more music. I don't know where it is going from here, but it is going somewhere." He admits that almost anything is worth a try. "You can't play God on what is going to work – all children are different, and even though it doesn't work the first time you should try it again. I don't know where technology is taking us, but you have to keep trying out the things that are coming through. Nobody gets into trouble for that, no matter how bizarre the plans might seem at the beginning – what we get into trouble for is not learning from them."

But Banes says that he has mixed feelings about technology. "There are two sides to it: being empowered but also being dependent. One of my concerns is if you actually bring together all that is possible with technology – a smart chair, a switching system that allows you to have full access, a communication machine – you have control of your environment, but end up as something like a Dalek. You can be in the centre of all this technology, but in there still is a human being with a need to socialise and interact. You could actually end up in a situation where you are so empowered that you no longer interact with people at a human level. If all your interactions are mediated by technology, what does that leave you with?"

❽ Higher Education

" **THE** idea of meeting to learn, to discover and to develop the imagination has been around since the beginnings of mankind – it's the meeting places that have changed." So said architect Sir Richard Rogers in 1996 when he unveiled a "beautiful barn of a building" he had designed for Thames Valley University in Slough. His sleek Learning Resource Centre is a new kind of meeting place in more ways than one, because it allows students to meet wherever they are.

▲　　▲　　▲

Even by today's changing standards, Thames Valley University (TVU) is an unusual seat of learning. Of its 29,000 students, 63 per cent are part-timers, and 89 per cent are over the age of 21. In full-time jobs, and often sponsored by their employers, they learn "with the university, not at it".

Those who come to the learning resource centre find a vast, open-plan space housing 150 computers. They can learn from CD-ROMs, publish essays, edit videos and research on the Internet, assisted by computer experts. There is a library of traditional print, policed by a new breed of librarian, who likes noise, in keeping with the university's view that learning is a social activity. But for those who cannot often make it to the campus, the computers and the people are at the heart of a network that reaches out to support students as they learn off-campus. Students link to e-mail students and lecturers, and use learning materials they are directed to by 'cyberlibrarians' who pull together information published on the Internet, on CD-ROMs, and in university databases. They turn it into learning material by adding comments and linking it to specific courses, then make it available in an electronic library.

One of the university's specialities is health sciences – TVU has incorporated several nursing colleges in recent years – and nurses have been among the first to benefit from the network. Andrew Ward, TVU's Head of Corporate Relations, says: "We have nurses and midwives coming from a whole range of hospitals so it is important to give them a way to access materials without having to come to the university. But you are actually taught as much through your fellow students as you are through a lecturer or a bunch of materials, so we are also trying to establish a community of learning. Go to the TVU Web site and you will see it work in practice – if a student asks a couple of other students a question, one person might come up with an answer, another will qualify that answer and then you might get a lecturer putting in a pennyworth as well."

Despite the hi-tech equipment, Ward says there are no plans to abandon face-to-face teaching. "All our indications are that a purely technology-driven education is not the answer. You can't just tell people: 'Everything is there, just press the button and that's it'. All our programmes involve lectures, and inspiring lecturers are always going to be important for stimulating the desire to learn. Our approach is multiple media, rather than multimedia. It may be that the best thing for you is an old fashioned book, or it may be an online database or an audio tape. In some institutions, the book is No.1 and everything else is a degraded version of it. In others, a little microsecond video bite is God. The old fashioned idea about reading for a degree should still exist. We don't want people to sound-bite for a degree."

The £4.2 million investment in the network and resources centre is being funded by TVU's commercial activities, in which the technology plays a crucial role. Corporate clients, including banks, ICT companies and manufacturers, hire the university to build electronic course materials and train staff. Even if employees are trained face-to-face, the TVU network ensures that they benefit from a community of learning once they are back at work. Nursing and midwifery courses count as commercial activity, says Ward, because the university has to bid competitively for the business to local health authorities. "We have moved from being an institution that made relatively little of its money through commercial activity to one that has just under 50 per cent from that source – that is, not given to us directly by the government. It is in our interest to increase it further, because that gives us more autonomy and freedom.

"It is an interesting dilemma. We want people to come to us to develop the skills of their workforce, but there are also students who come in full time. People here have to recognise that when someone crosses the doorstep, whether they are there for 25 minutes to pick up a lecture or for four years to do an undergraduate degree, they are a student and must be treated accordingly, on a par. Almost every university has some commercial activity, but where we are different is that we have had to grow from a weakness. Most universities have technology, engineering, or science faculties – research or technology transfer departments, with something they can sell on. But we are a teaching and learning institution, so we have had to go about things in a completely different way. Commercialising the university is not something that is done on the side, a little option to buy one or two computers – it is essential to the way we go about everything."

THE POLYVERSITY

The idea that higher education is a full-time pursuit for 18-21-year-old school-leavers is dead. Of the 1.6 million students in higher education, almost one third are studying on part-time courses. Higher Education Statistics Agency figures for the year 1996/7 show that 56 per cent of all new students were mature on entry, and 29 per cent of new students for full-time first degree courses fell into the mature category. Thanks to the recommendations of three government-appointed groups – Helena Kennedy's Widening Participation Committee (further education), Sir Ron Dearing's Committee of Enquiry (higher education) and Professor Bob Fryer's National Advisory Group on Continuing Education and Lifelong Learning – the student profile is set to change even more dramatically. Universities and colleges will be competing to attract a wider audience. But they will also have to co-operate, as students will expect to be able to mix and match academic and vocational qualifications at various staging posts throughout their lives. The boundaries between work, education and training will become increasingly blurred. And as the workforce becomes more mobile, and work more international, learning will become a global affair, with the expectation that qualifications be recognised around the world. As Mary Lord of the Training and Enterprise Council (TEC) National Council put it in an address to a TEC Lifelong Learning Conference: "Instead of a university, we could end up with a global polyversity."

Technology presents both a threat and an opportunity. Thanks to the Internet, anyone can muscle in as an education provider, selling and delivering online courses anywhere in the world, for very little investment. There are campus-free virtual universities, which put up all their courses and converse with students on the Internet. Thousands of courses, covering everything from engineering to embalming, are available online from a whole host of vendors, from bona fide institutions to one-man bands. Even companies are joining the fray, using education as a corporate marketing tool by building Internet learning centres where potential customers can take management training and professional development courses at no cost.

Britain's universities and colleges have already begun to respond, using distance learning and the Internet as the way of reaching a wider audience. A visit to the Online Education Web site, for example, which markets MBAs via distance-learning to students in Hong Kong, reveals that the courseware and degree are from the University of Paisley in Scotland. Several virtual universities are now being run in the UK, in attempts by universities and colleges to broaden their net, and provide better service to specific sectors of the market. The most high-profile is in the Highlands and Islands region of Scotland, an area the size of Belgium, which has been campaigning for its own university for a century. Building on the success of an educational network called First Class that links all the area's schools, the region decided to link colleges into the network and grow a university for itself. The new University of The Highlands and Islands offered its first distance-learning course, a BSc in Rural Development, to the world via the Internet in 1997.

The Dearing Committee of Inquiry report recommended that by 2005 every student should be required to have a laptop computer. Many students are already Internet-literate, thanks to free access to the Net via JANET, the UK network that links all the country's universities plus colleges and affiliated organisations. JANET is currently being transformed into SUPERJANET, an upgraded network that handles more traffic and videoconferencing, and which incorporates very-high-speed regional networks, called MANs (metropolitan area networks) which link higher education institutions located closely together. SUPERJANET will make it easier to network large quantities of research data, library texts, and multimedia course material between institutions. Through links to the National Grid for Learning it will be easier to reach students, at home, in libraries or at work. It seems inevitable that more and more students will become distance-learners. What needs to happen to make to make this a success for both tutor and student? The technology is here today – current work is focused on how to apply it well.

THE OPEN UNIVERSITY

One of the most successful distance learning organisations in the world is the UK's Open University. Since it began teaching in 1971, 2.5 million people have studied on one of its courses. Now the country's largest university, it currently has 160,000 students, representing 23 per cent of all people studying in part-time higher education. The original concept was a University of the Air, which would allow adults to study in their own homes, courtesy of television and radio broadcasts and correspondence courses. Today, as well as reaching out to students in 100 countries with courses, degrees and diplomas on everything from computing to community affairs, the university has one of the largest business schools in Europe and is rated highly for its research.

In fact broadcasting has served only as the icing on the cake, enticing students, enhancing their learning, but never acting as a major delivery medium. And face-to-face contact – meetings with local tutors and summer school gatherings – has always been important. The university created its first electronic campus – a way for students to take part in online conferences – as far back as 1988. But it has resisted the temptation to rush headlong into making online courses the norm. With a wide range of students (from a nine-year-old maths prodigy to a 93-year-old graduate) with different backgrounds and lifestyles, some of whom have not studied for decades, or have never studied before, it uses a wide range of media, from books and audiotapes to computer-based texts. As it says: "We don't pin our reputation on the latest electronic gadget, or the size of our bandwidth, but on how well our students learn."

Dr Robin Mason, head of the Centre for Information Technology in Education (CITE) at the OU's Institute of Educational Technology, says: "We have nearly 40,000 students online. Lots of courses use computers, but fewer use access to the Internet. There are only 10-15 courses for which it is obligatory to have access to our student conferences, but many in which it is voluntary and lots of students carry on using the system amongst themselves."

The computer conference allows everyone to take part in a discussion, without all having to be online at the same time – people simply e-mail their contributions to a communal conference area for others to pick up. Dr Mason says: "We try to promote the notion of a discussion rather than a question-and-answer session where the tutor is the fount of all knowledge. It is more valuable to have a discussion where everyone contributes and the tutor may be more of a guide, more experienced and more knowledgeable but still one of the contributors. It gives people the opportunity to express their own opinions. Some of our students are experts in their own field and contribute from their own base of experience – sometimes they are more expert in one particular field than the tutor. Many students also write summaries of articles from magazines, interesting and up-to-date titbits as a resource for everyone on the course."

Dr Mason says the university is now working on ways to make conferencing activities an integral part of a course, with students being assessed on their contributions. One approach involves setting an essay question, and allowing a group of 20 students to discuss the subject online, sending in their messages to the conferencing system. Each student then has to select his or her best messages and send them to the tutor. Marks are based on the extent to which students comment on others' contributions, and on how they use material from the course in their messages. "We feel this helps to build the skills of taking other people's views and learning to comment on them," says Dr Mason.

Students studying for a Master's degree in open and distance learning, run by the Institute, already have all their assignments linked through the conferencing system, and do collaborative work such as writing joint reports. But Dr Mason says: "This is a graduate course, relatively small and easy to manage. There are problems with trying to work collaboratively at undergraduate level on a mass scale, although we are interested in trying more discussions."

Other online activities include role-playing exercises in which students act out an event through the eyes of different characters. In an experimental course on renewable energy, they became players in a legal wrangle over building a windfarm on the outskirts of a village – judge, residents, developers and newspaper reporters all expressed their conflicting positions via a conference. Dr Mason feels it is also important to punctuate courses with 'real-time' discussions and lectures between people who arrange to be online at the same time. "It is very easy to get dispirited in a course that is done totally online. People need some real-time activity to keep them motivated and to add real presence." She says that with the rise of the Web, collaborative learning is becoming increasingly important, but: "My guess is it would never form more than a small percentage of courses because it is hard to mark and hard work for students – just very demanding at every level. It is exciting and dynamic, but expensive and labour intensive. Inevitably something like that only rolls out in a very weakened-down form." She is currently working on a guide to best practice for teaching online, and helping tutors get to grips with the technology. But she says: "The problems are never with the technology, really – they are always social and inter-personal."

THE VICARIOUS LEARNER

Conferencing helps overcome the loneliness of the long-distance learner – the feeling of isolation that can cause people's confidence to flag. Students find that other people have similar questions and difficulties to their own, and benefit from listening in to other people's discussions. But if these exchanges are valuable, shouldn't they be saved and made available to future generations of students? That is the thinking behind The Vicarious Learner project, run by Professor Terry Mayes of the Centre for Teaching and Learning Innovation at Glasgow Caledonian University.

He says: "In traditional teaching, learning experiences were always transient. As electronic learning becomes increasingly common, people are keeping all sorts of records which previously would have just vanished from year to year. One of our basic ideas is to take the electronic products of learning episodes and structure them into a new kind of courseware, to find out whether they are valuable for new learners. One of the most obvious applications is in online learning." The scheme is being tried out in a variety of courses, including one in which four Scottish universities – Glasgow, Glasgow Caledonian, Heriot Watt and Napier – are sharing resources to teach one course over metropolitan area networks.

As well as capturing online conference discussions, the project is video-recording tutorials and linking videoclips to primary course material. Frequently-asked questions (FAQs) are also put in a database. If students don't find the answer they are looking for in the database, their question is routed to a tutor, who replies and decides whether the question is worthy of being added to the list of FAQs. Professor Mayes says: "In distance learning courses in more discursive subjects, being able to access discussions of other students might compensate for the lack of face-to-face dialogue. But it is a complex subject – and dialogue for a mathematician would be different from that of a historian."

He began investigating vicarious learning in 1990. "I saw that linking traditional subject matter with communications was a powerful concept that wasn't exploited properly – the whole area was being dominated by the simple idea of multimedia content. A postgraduate student pointed to a conference paper from the USA about the Answer Garden, a piece of software aimed at organisational memory. Companies were trying to build a database of questions and answers that captured the expertise of their employees, which is particularly valuable when you have people who leave and take valuable expertise to a competitor. I saw immediately that there could be an educational application too."

The idea is to be tried out in schools ("It might be useful for people who don't ask questions in class") and Professor Mayes believes it could also prove invaluable for company employees such as service engineers and customer support staff who need answers to questions at times when their organisations are often too stretched to offer answers.

THE VIRTUAL TUTORIAL

Alistair Kelman describes himself as "a barrister with attitude". He specialises in intellectual property law, runs a computer consultancy, and is also a Visiting Fellow at the London School of Economics (LSE), where he teaches a postgraduate course in Information Systems and the Law. As if that were not enough to keep him occupied, Kelman is now running virtual tutorials with his students, in an attempt to find out how distance learning could be used at LSE in future. The move was partly driven by his professional travels around Europe and the USA, which meant that lectures were sometimes cancelled at short notice. But turning up to tutorials is also an expensive business for students, and, since most have computers and Internet access at home, and already correspond with Kelman by e-mail, it made sense to try an online approach. Students are equipped with software that allows them to type and read messages at leisure, only running up phone bills when they connect to the online tutorial area to post or collect messages.

One recent tutorial involved 20 people, including students in India and the head of the legal advisory board of the European Commission in Luxembourg, who was sitting in on the exercise. First, the students were given a list of Web site addresses where they could do some reading in advance. They were then asked a question – "Is taxation of the Internet inevitable?" – to which they had to answer simply yes or no. Depending on the answer they gave, they were then directed to other material, and asked supplementary questions. If they answered 'no', for instance, they had to suggest alternative ways in which government taxation revenues would be maintained. For five days, no-one was allowed to post answers, which gave people time to reflect and research, and when they did come up with their conclusions, they were available for everyone to comment on.

Kelman says: "A lot of problems with these electronic exercises is that you don't know at the end of them whether you've finished – you just go on and on and on. The tutor has to be very proactive in the discussion, and it needs people at the highest level to really work on the tutorials. An experienced lecturer will be able to tell what is nonsense from what is genius. Sometimes you have got to let kids with good ideas run on, while at other times you've got to shut them up because it is not taking the discussion anywhere. We also need a disciplinary code because when the students are not physically together, some of them cause trouble with unnecessary comments. Some peer pressure has to be exerted on them in some way."

There is also an issue with the fact that everything in a tutorial is recorded. "If students know that everything they are going to say in a tutorial is going to be reviewed and stored for all time it is going to inhibit them from making fools of themselves. You have to make a fool of yourself if you are going to learn."

So far, Kelman says the scheme has been an unqualified success, but, despite the fact that he has put some of his lectures online, he has no plans to run an entirely virtual course. "I think that is going to be very difficult to do. You must have some experience of working with the people and you can amplify and develop that with virtual teaching, but you can't do it totally hands off. What I would like to be able to do is give an introductory lecture to the students, and then follow-up lectures would be given virtually. That way the student has built the relationship with me and by the time he hears the virtual lecture, radio-with-pictures, he knows my gestures and can visualise me giving the lecture. He is not staring out of the window, and not suffering from indigestion or a hangover – and if he is, he can take the lecture again. At the end he can take part in the virtual tutorial. The effort is twofold. What is essential in any course development of this sort is that students don't just learn a bunch of facts, but that they learn to think like lawyers – or engineers, scientists or economists. It is teaching people to think, not just to know.

"I really see the future of this as not so much getting rid of physical teaching, but actually shortening a degree from three years down to 18 months, and staggering it over time, with the student coming in and seeing his friends, then going away, back into work, and developing in a work environment. It is a bit more like the old sandwich courses, but a lot more telescoped. I am also seeing how this programme could work very well using young practising barristers as the law tutors. They are hanging around in court, waiting for cases to come on. Most of them today have laptop computers – they shouldn't have any problem devoting an hour or two a day to tutoring while their practice is building up. That would mean you have people with practical experience able to educate and teach – and earn a little money as well."

LEGAL ISSUES

Kelman says there are some interesting legal questions raised by the virtual tutorials. One is how to protect the privacy of students, given that all online exchanges are recorded. "Supposing that, three years from now, we've got Prince William in a class, and he starts questioning certain aspects of government policy. Now, that becomes a news story. If someone has sat in a tutorial at the LSE and is questioning certain political shibboleths and then later on runs for political office – and it does happen at the LSE – you want to ensure that the privacy of their communications is kept secret. And yet you need to be able to reuse this material and build the trust relationship between the lecturer and the student. I consider that to be the most difficult problem we have to face

– the anonymising and protection of students' privacy, and their 'right to be wrong'."

He says that lecturers also need to be careful how they use material from the Web in their courses. "If I got on to a Web site and saw an article that was interesting, then copied it to all the students, that would be an illegal act. If I want to copy documents and give them to other people I must get permission from the copyright owners. But if I just give the student the URL (the Web site address), the student can go and download it for himself, just as he would do if he was going to the library and looking at a work for himself. That is considered fair use under the law. Considerable work is going on within universities in developing course packs, and they have to pay royalties to the various authors. This way we can create an electronic course pack – a series of clicking things – where you don't have to pay a penny. And that means that we can reduce the cost of education."

This approach founders, however, when Web publishers decide to charge users for access to their sites. This is becoming increasingly common, as Internet security is stepped up and consumers feel happier about giving out credit card numbers over the Net. Kelman recently gave students a reference to one well-known site which later decided to charge a 'pay per view' fee for every page read. "I tried to negotiate with them but they said we had to pay some silly figure. As we develop courses, we are going to have to negotiate a series of deals on behalf of the school, to stop people closing off Web sites just when we want to use their material. Once we know how many people are on the course, we can come up with a proper calculation."

So with universities publishing courseware on the Web, how do they protect their own copyright? Some choose to protect their material by giving students passwords, others give Web users free use to material, only paying when they want a qualification. Kelman says that one of the most interesting approaches he has seen is to link a book to a Web site.

Buy the book, and it gives you the password to get on to the Web site, where there is additional material. "I see that as the model for the future – academic textbooks are going to be linked to Web sites. University institutions will say: 'You buy this course pack and it gives you access to this Web site'. And at the end of the day, you pay your examination fees and get your degree."

LINKING WORLD RESEARCH

Ever-more powerful computers and the Internet are making possible research which previously could only be dreamed of, but technology also has its drawbacks. The Roslin Institute in Edinburgh, famous for cloning Dolly the sheep, is a major player in the international effort to map livestock genomes. Although the more famous Human Genome Project aims to sequence the whole of the human DNA code, this is not financially viable for farm animals, so the project aims to put some markers on the genetic maps of various breeds of livestock and make comparisons – compare, say, the pig map with the human map. The information is held in databases that can be created and interrogated anywhere in the world. Roslin is responsible for holding summary databases for the international effort on the pig and chicken genome, and for developing tools to help analyse databases for other livestock. Roslin's Dr Harry Griffin says: "You need to be able to interrogate information and you need the special bioinformatic tools that allow you to make comparisons easily. It is not merely a collation of information but a synthesis of information from all kinds of sources. There is no way that this could be done by anything other than bioinformatics and by easy computer links between the various groups working in these areas."

He says the Internet has benefits and drawbacks. "You can be exceedingly well-informed these days. If you are an active scientist, you tend to stick to the same journals – 10 or 20 is probably the most that you can trawl through. But with computer-based retrieval systems you can systematically search the scientific literature and find papers that might be relevant in rather obscure journals. To some extent you can end up with information overload."

"There is another element. In genetics and genome analysis, because the task is large and the effort is international, most of the information appears to be out in the public domain, and certainly at the moment that is the case. There is a belief that when it comes to creating these genome maps it is very important that the information should be easily shared, because any one group can only contribute a small fraction of the total effort required – if you need say 1,000 markers spread across 26 chromosomes, even a fairly large organisation can contribute only 20-40 of these. But one of the criticisms from funding bodies is: 'The UK government are paying for this; what is UK PLC specifically getting out of it – aren't we just giving this information to all and sundry?'

"It is in the next phase, when we begin to use these maps to identify where genes of commercial importance are located, that you get back to being able to create some sort of competitive advantage – some of our work is funded by a consortium of pig-breeding companies. There is always a dilemma about freely publishing material, and with the Internet, publishing is almost instantaneous. But it is really more about the application, once you have got the basic map, how you use that information in breeding programmes, in identifying genes of major importance in commercial breeds and flocks. It is then that you would go back into an element of commercial confidence, and be able to gain commercial advantage for the UK by ensuring that the industry and academic community – including ourselves – are working much more closely together than they might do."

Dolly caused a barrage of public interest, much of it via the Internet. Dr Griffin says: "The single most active category of e-mail requests was from American high school and college kids wanting to update their latest assignment. We couldn't easily cope with that. We upgraded our Web site – there are some articles on cloning – and we're using it to provide background information for journalists. Certainly the public and the Press need more education. In the case of Dolly, the public were much more sanguine – the Press milked it for what it was worth. A lot of the fears they imagined were plucked from science fiction. I think we will increasingly use the Internet as a way of getting information across."

As far as schools go, Roslin is currently working out what role it might have in the advanced biology curriculum and a new senior biotechnology course due to start in Scotland in the year 2000. Dr Griffin says: "There is quite a lot in there that is relevant or describes work that we are doing. It would be nice to think we could educate the next generation about biotechnology, and make them want to be scientists. We have had some experience talking to schools, and because our sheep have been so well exposed to the media, getting the science behind it over to the kids seems to work very effectively – like trying to explain animation using Mickey Mouse. But we are not into public education – until Dolly we were relatively obscure and purposely so. There are plenty of opportunities for expanding into public understanding of science through Dolly, but whether we have the resources to achieve it is another matter."

9 Wider Education

"**WE** lost our jobs, we lost our skills, we lost our school. We have had too many defeats – now we need a success." Derek Garrity speaks for the people of Aylesham in Kent, a community whose recent history makes a depressing story. Aylesham was a thriving mining village until the closure of the Kent coalfields began in 1969. Its local pit was closed in 1988, creating mass unemployment. Men who found work were later laid off when the Channel Tunnel was completed, and when dockyard workforces were cut back. In 1992 the secondary school was shut down, and the children were bussed out to other towns. Derek Garrity says: "One of our two primary schools failed the OFSTED test, and is being run under special measures, so basically we now have an educational problem from start to finish."

▲　　▲　　▲

In 1993, Garrity, a miner's son who trained as an electrician, started to investigate what plans the authorities had for the village. The answer was none, so he came up with a scheme of his own, to re-open the secondary school and use it as a community training centre. After months of hawking the plan around the authorities, he secured funding from various sponsors, formed the Aylesham District Community Workshop Trust, and re-opened the school in late 1997. Today it hosts shops and offices for small businesses, runs courses and workshops given by local colleges, and boasts a computer-equipped telecentre, which has become the focal point on which many local people are pinning their hopes for the future. "People see the computers as a way of getting new skills for new jobs," says Garrity.

He says that people used to go on half-day-a-week college computer courses in other towns, but because no-one had a home PC, they didn't get any practice from one week to the next. Learners at Aylesford can now join a computer club that gives them access to machines in their spare time. Schoolchildren also come in for an afternoon a week, because at the two schools, 440 pupils have only four ancient machines between them. Garrity feels computers can help adults who have problems with literacy and numeracy: "Many people round here didn't have very good educational experiences, but with a computer it doesn't matter if you can't spell or can't think of a word or add or subtract. If you can teach someone how to format a piece of work it looks good and can give them self-pride."

Requests for success stories, however, don't go down well with Garrity. He says: "The way we look at it, there have been 30 years of decline, and we have only been here for a few months. I don't want to start claiming successes, and I don't want a five-minute wonder." The Trust has secured £700,000 funding and a nominal school rent of £1 a year, but Garrity warns that the project needs to be sustained: "When the great and the good come here I say: 'If you come here once, you are not going to make a big impact. And if you give us money, don't just give us one batch of money and leave us – you might as well give us nothing.' I know it is going to take 20 years to build up the skills again. There are no guarantees here – you can work hard and still be unemployed. But what we are telling people is that maybe learning a bit of IT and a bit of other things might help, even if it is only to fill in your dole form."

UNIVERSITY FOR INDUSTRY

The Kent miners indicate the nature of the task that faces the government's University For Industry (UFI). As a broker between potential learners and all kinds of training organisations – colleges, universities, companies, unions, voluntary groups – UFI promises to make learning more accessible for people from all walks of life, from chief executives too frightened to admit they need training, to housewives at home who think they aren't worthy of it. Dubbed "the biggest and most radical education initiative anywhere in the world", it paves the way for a more flexible system of personally-tailored education, whereby adults can mix and match qualifications, and dip in and out of training as their needs and training budgets dictate. But part of the UFI's role will also be to draw in potential customers by marketing the whole idea of learning. The first UFI pilot, begun in north-east England in late 1997, is testing possible marketing approaches.

Computers and the Internet are proving a great draw. The most high profile activity takes place at the Sunderland Football Ground, the Stadium of Light, where the University of Sunderland runs its specially-designed course, A Football Fan's Guide to the Internet, and where whole families come along to search football Web sites and send e-mail to star players. Other course venues include schools, colleges, libraries, and the Metro Centre in Gateshead, and most courses have elements that can be done at home or work. Helen Milner, project manager for the pilot, says: "We are trying to say: 'Learning is a normal part of your life, so it happens where you norm:ally go'."

Potential learners can ring a freephone advice line, or apply via the Web. There are 'taster' courses on offer to tempt people in, and ICT is proving by far the most popular subject. Applicants for IT For The Terrified receive a book and a CD-ROM, and are assigned a tutor from a local college or university who is available at certain times at a local learning centre. Helen says that most people don't arrange to meet the tutor – they either work through the book or go along and get straight on to the PC. On a recent family Internet treasure hunt, adults were sent a taster workbook before they came along. Helen says: "The book was designed to use with the Internet, but most people had read it cover to cover before they arrived. Some said they were only here because their children wanted to come, but within half an hour they were scrolling about the screen and asking about courses, which was the whole point of it."

Two months into the pilot, 600 people had registered for courses, of whom around half were unemployed. Helen says: "We have a database with all the records of everybody who inquires, everybody who registers, what they are doing, and where and when they are doing it, so that we can monitor progression and the different courses people are taking. We will use that to send them information about new courses that they might be interested in." She says that UFI is also marketing to small businesses, although targeting individuals in companies has been a more successful tack. Various professional skills courses are on offer, and run on demand.

Some employers, such as the National Health Service, have joined the scheme. At the NHS training centre in Sunderland General Hospital, domestics and consultants sit side-by-side at computers taking personal development courses. Although no training providers have put their materials online, learners can e-mail tutors and join in online conferences from home, work or any of the learning centres. Helen says: "Part of the UFI's role will be to help providers change the way they deliver education and training, based on what the market wants. So if small businesses say what they really need is more information about exporting to Europe in an online database, then UFI will tell providers that is what they want."

She says: "Industry in its loosest sense means the workforce, and UFI is about employability for those in work and out of work. The aim behind it is to make our workforce more competitive. Even if you are employed and a graduate, UFI is for you. We have people registered for a whole range of levels of courses in a whole range of ways – ones which suit them. You may be an employed graduate but you might not have done any learning for 15 years. UFI is about coming back throughout your life for bits of learning."

ATTITUDES TO LEARNING

Given that the UFI plans to use existing resources wherever possible, how can training providers serve a wider audience? They need to be able to reach everybody, including reluctant learners. At Kent Training and Enterprise Council (TEC), research is underway to identify different people's attitudes to learning, and experimentation with products that work for them is being undertaken. Kent TEC has a 10-year strategy for lifelong learning, which is woven through all its activities, from encouraging women to go back to work to helping businesses be more competitive. Annual targets – from the number of adults who have personal learning plans to the number of teachers seconded to companies – are monitored by the Kent Forum for Lifelong Learning, set up in 1995 by the TEC, the County Council and the county's Association of Further Education Colleges. At its Web site, the TEC brings together and demystifies all the options that are available. There is a strong emphasis on learning in (or for) employment, and on boosting Kent's economy for the good of everyone who lives there.

In 1994, work started to try to identify different attitudes to training. Sharon Copestake, Senior Research Executive, says: "We clustered people together and identified groups, from those who had had enough at school and never wanted to go near it again, to the people who couldn't get enough of it. We have also done a lot of research on barriers to learning. For example, everybody says 'accessibility' – for me that could mean having a course on the Internet, for you it might mean having your three children cared for or taken to school. We are discovering that it is not as black and white as people care to think. We are in this age of individualism, and people don't like to be categorised; it is about meeting personal and individual needs."

Groups were then targeted with different approaches. One of the most successful campaigns is aimed at women with low confidence, who have been out of the job market for some time. Sharon says: "We don't sell the idea of 'learning', but we talk about confidence-building, self-awareness and presentation. There is a women returners' network which runs group seminars in which women can discuss their personal experiences and learn from one another to build up confidence to decide to go back to work. Once we get to that stage we say: 'These are your opportunities – what can we do to make these happen?'" For the disillusioned, it seems that informal approaches work best. An Open Minds campaign run on TV and radio, aimed at encouraging people to ring an advice line, produced few leads, while schemes that use family links or community networks are proving successful. In Ashford in Kent, courses in a family learning centre, with free child care, were advertised by giving children leaflets to take home from school. Many parents turned up with two or three neighbours. And a mobile Learning Bus, equipped with PCs, provides another change of scene for people who shun traditional classrooms.

Kent TEC has also found that today's learners see themselves as customers, who want to learn when and where they choose, and technology is a way of giving them more control. Community centres around the county – Derek Garrity's in Aylesham is one – are being equipped as telecentres in which people can learn from courses on the Internet, and contact tutors or advisers by videoconferencing. One centre employs videoconferencing to enable deaf people to sign to remote advisers. Another encourages people who have had mental health problems to come in and use multimedia software to learn at their own pace, rather then being overwhelmed in a busy college classroom. Each centre has a different aim, but all are run by local people, whom learners will have met in shops or pubs. Sunil Kumar, who runs IT projects for Kent TEC, says: "The courses aren't like professional ones which charge people £300 a day to learn about word-processing. You may pay £1 for a visit to a centre, but you can spend all day there, so you are not pressurised into doing things and then coming up against a barrier and never coming back again. Lots of people go along because they need to write a CV. They learn how to word-process, and maybe how to use a spreadsheet. Then they might use a CD-ROM to learn French, and look for information that interests them on the Internet. But the majority – the core users – are using the centre to acquire the IT skills they need to get a job."

Kent TEC is now reviewing the original groups of learners it identified, to see whether its efforts have had an effect. Sharon Copestake says: "I am hoping to track the very disillusioned people to see whether you can actually change attitudes to learning, as it is quite hard to do."

Work is also going on to build in the results of research done by Lyndon West at the University of Kent, who carried out a five-year study with students to find out how their view of themselves varied over time, and how their personal history affected decisions. Kent TEC's Steve Matthews says: "It has a bearing on advice and guidance. People often go along to an interview and say: 'I want to be a radiographer, because I think it is a good steady job', whereas in fact there is often a personal biographical detail many years back which is the subliminal decider on where they are going. Things happen in their family, in their personal lives, and maybe the view we take of how people make decisions is a bit simplistic." Any Kent resident who doesn't have access to advice through work or further education is eligible for a voucher that buys time with one of 17 different organisations who can help put together a personal learning plan. Steve says: "The idea is that it is demand-driven, and the individual has purchasing power."

Of the UFI, he says: "It is a great opportunity, but there is an awful lot going on that needs to be pulled together. The trend is towards learning on demand and how you modify the supply side to make it provide that. The shortage of funding means that you are constantly looking at driving down costs using the existing resources. That is a key message of the UFI – we are not looking at a major monster investment in brand new things, it is actually pulling together existing provision, kite-marking it, and then the money goes into development of high-tech, very user-friendly multimedia resources, which two or three years from now may appear on PlayStations rather than PCs!"

TECHNO-FEAR

PlayStations or not, many people are still scared of technology. "One woman could barely walk into the room, she was so frightened," says Heather Holyhead, who gives Computing for the Terrified courses in Staffordshire, and this is echoed by teachers around the country. In companies, people are often handed expensive equipment and just left to get on with it. Some senior managers defeat the purpose of the communications revolution by asking secretaries to print out all their e-mail and stack it up in the in-tray, where it lies for days. At South Bristol Learning Network (SBLN), Maurice King *(see page 10)* and his colleagues are masters of the art of overcoming techno-fear. The trademark of their Cyberskills workshops is removal of the mystifying jargon ("this a course about writing, not pens"). They concentrate on why people have come along to learn about computers and the Internet. The most successful part of the half-day workshop, given to everyone from small businesses to the Women's Institute, is a group discussion at the end where everyone talks about how they can help one another beyond the course. The point is to build up a human network as well as an electronic one. SBLN's Sally Abram says: "There is still a huge amount of techno-fear about, even though some of the jargon is beginning to be part of mainstream conversation. People from all walks of life are now talking about the Internet, but they don't really know what it is. They are scared to admit it. The reason we have been so successful is that we aren't teccies – it's very relaxed." She says that SBLN staff were hired because they had interests outside work, and "a glint in their eye".

With the help of ICL, the Cyberskills formula was packaged, and is now being franchised by the Cyberskills Association to CyberSkills Development Agencies operating around the world. They range from community groups to further education organisations. SBLN continues to develop courses for The Cyberskills Association, and all material is being accredited through the open college network. The Association is also exploring how European and American accreditation might work.

LEARNING AT WORK

SBLN itself has turned its attention to small businesses, which traditionally have a severe problem finding the time and resources to train staff. (And even if they do have the time, putting together a course themselves for only five or ten employees is a prohibitively expensive luxury.) Workshops introduce firms to the essential ICT skills for their business, and how to use the Internet to promote themselves. Sally Abram says: "We find that small businesses aren't terribly interested in getting a qualification at the end of it. The experience for the individuals is more important: what new skills are they getting out of it, and how can they apply them at work?" SBLN is now running a business network. For a £25 fee, members receive nine hours of training, access to SBLN computer workshops at evenings and weekends, and help-desk support. Sally says: "On a lot of courses, people go for a day, then go away, and they are left to sink or swim. We are trying to give them a support system – if the issues are about access, for example, well, we can provide it here. And we can often advise on what support or funding for small businesses is coming down the line."

Larger companies, often suffering from downsizing exercises which removed a whole raft of experienced personnel, are now starting to realise the value of helping their staff to learn. Some have become 'learning organisations', changing their entire culture so that the whole company can quickly learn from, and react to, individual employees' experiences (including mistakes). 'Knowledge officers' are being appointed to make this happen. Intranets help staff to work collaboratively, and to learn from each other. (A company Intranet is like the firm's own Internet – it contains private information and is used only by the employees of the company and perhaps related organisations such as suppliers or customers). In the USA, over 1,000 companies have established their own corporate universities, some with their own campuses. The idea is to cut the cost of sending people on external courses, and ensure that they learn in the context of their own jobs. But however they tackle the problem of training, there is a common thread running through their strategy: companies are realising that because the climate is changing so fast, their staff need to learn how to learn.

Andrew Ward of Thames Valley University says: "Companies are beginning to think that learning breeds learning. People might come along to us to study something that might not seem to be related to their job. A company in Slough is sending its staff to our Learning Resource Centre to do self-paced mini-modules on anything that interests them – one man has been enquiring about Polish – but actually what it is doing is keeping them tuned up and enthusiastic. The logic is that if you can manage your own learning about something that interests you, then you can go back to the workplace and self-manage your own development to a certain degree." He says that corporate activity will shape the nature of qualifications in the years to come: "It may well be that we see some very interesting joint degrees. The classic area would be in retailing, where we have the absurd situation where a student does a 3-4 year degree and then a further year's training to be a retail manager. Why don't we get together, treat some of that training as modules and accredit them so that when the student leaves, they have a degree but also the qualifications that will equip them to be a retail manager?"

He sees ICT skilling as important: "It is still the case that there are very senior people in companies who are technophobic. It needs diplomacy and deft delicacy in trying to help people at that level." But he says that ICT fanatics can also be a liability. "There is a real problem with people who are addicted to surfing. They go into work and they are hooked on it. The information goes on to disk or paper and is never read by anyone – people are just hoarding it. That's what we want to avoid with learning. We want people to use technology rather than technology using them. Anyone can go and get information, but it is being able to process it and turn it into knowledge that counts."

TRAINING ON THE NET

Peritas is the UK's largest training company, and specialises in corporate training, particularly in the use of ICT. For years it has been training in the classroom, but for many companies this is impractical. A recent challenge, for example, was presented by the Scottish Prisons Service. In the space of six months, it had to train 4500 officers how to use a new computer records system to log prisoners. The majority had little experience of computers, and, of course, they couldn't leave their posts *en masse*. Peritas designed a distance-learning program which combined small workshops with the use of a specially-designed multimedia software. The software mimicked the officers' work environment, and employed humour – such as cartoons of real-life officers – to put first-time computer users at their ease.

Peritas has been designing distance learning software for years, and launched training on the Internet in 1995; anyone with a credit card could sign up to learn. Shortly afterwards it became a pioneer member of the Microsoft Online Institute, designed to train people in the use of

Microsoft software. Peritas' managing director, Paul Butler, says: "When we launched, people said: 'Who on earth is going to want training on the Internet?' Today, we have students from as far away as Sydney and Nicaragua."

To make a success of distance learning, says Butler, you have not only to provide the materials, but also to add the things that make classroom teaching work: interaction, motivation and discipline. Without these, there are just too many distractions at work and at home that threaten to sabotage the learner's efforts. "The classroom is the perfect environment in which to use technology. Students writing a program, for example, can try things out, ask questions and get an immediate answer, listen to other people. Interaction with peers is immensely valuable – you compare notes, experiences, in the class or at break times. You also have discipline, because the tutor drives the class to complete the work in a certain time."

Every student who signs up with Peritas is assigned a tutor, who e-mails the student a schedule for the course – how long it will take, and the self-study deadlines that have to be met for periodic tests which will arrive by e-mail. After each test, the tutor advises the student of areas that require more work, and may recommend more exercises or reading. Students can also log on and chat to the tutor and the rest of the class at pre-arranged times. Proof that this approach works came in the form of an eye-opening exercise which Peritas was asked to do recently, when two companies which had merged required ICT training. One group of 60 opted for the tutor-driven approach; the other group said it just wanted to give its 35 people "a bunch of disks". Of the first group, 4 people dropped out, and 87 per cent of the remainder passed the exam first time, after 7 weeks. The second group had 12 weeks in which to study, but only 5 per cent passed the exam first time. "The second figure is a fairly typical figure," says Butler. "We know that, because we deal with companies which set up learning centres filled with multimedia, but they are seldom used. People are busy with their jobs and private lives and no one is driving them." In future Butler sees the company as being able to help students with their personal training portfolio, including everything from gardening to painting.

INCLUSIVE LEARNING

For Britain's lifelong learners, the future could look like this. Everyone will be armed with electronic smart cards, giving access to advice and education from home or work, at a variety of venues ranging from libraries to pubs. The intelligent plastic cards will be loaded with a personal career and training history, as well as training credits – entitlements to training that are bought by individuals, or contributed by employers and the government. Learners will be able to slide the card into a computer or other device and connect to the National Grid For Learning, and pay for their training, which will be increasingly delivered online if the subject is suited to it. Net computers – stripped-down computers that download most of the software they need to operate from the Internet – are one example of how it is becoming cheaper to equip people to use the Net. One wit predicted that it would soon be possible to surf the Net from a toaster. The arrival of digital broadcasting will also provide another powerful medium, with almost unlimited channels and the ability for the viewer to interact with programmes. As all this technology converges – as is happening – people should have to worry less about operating the equipment and should be able to concentrate more on content and intent.

Who stands at risk of being excluded? In theory, no-one; in practice, it depends on just how far the tentacles of the Grid reach out. Will they extend to Britain's prisons, for example? Research has shown strong links between educational failure and crime; one study has shown that 40 per cent of prison inmates have some kind of learning difficulty.

And for homeless people – although it doesn't solve their major problems – one of the simplest ideas was to offer people individual e-mail addresses, so that with the aid of publicly-available Internet access, they at least had their own address where they could be reached by friends and which they could give to prospective employers. The scheme has been tried in the USA, but in Britain, even though it is now possible to buy an e-mail address for life without buying access to the Internet, the idea has been slow to take off.

⑩ Libraries and Museums

PHILANTHROPIST Andrew Carnegie

spent $60 million funding 2,811 libraries in the passionate belief that books, the key to self-improvement, should be available free to every citizen. Today, Angela McCormick at the Carnegie Library in Ayr says: "If Andrew Carnegie was to establish libraries now, access to computers would be as important as access to books."

▲   ▲   ▲

She argues that computer literacy and information from the Internet are just as crucial today as literacy and access to the printed word were 100 years ago when the first Carnegie libraries opened. As IT co-ordinator for South Ayrshire Libraries, she is blazing a trail that a modern-day Carnegie would be proud of.

The Carnegie library has a CyberCentre, now being cloned in branch libraries. Staffed by a librarian and two assistants, and equipped with ranks of computers, it sits in an open-plan area. "Silence in public libraries is somewhat outmoded," says Angela, "although there should always be a quiet room for reading. A library should be the hub of the community." Funds from the book budget were diverted to buy the equipment. "People were horrified – librarians sucked air between their teeth. But I feel quite strongly that we have to make this available because people are disadvantaged if they don't have access to computers."

As a result, she says, people of all ages have been coming in "in droves", from children using CD-ROMs to elderly people who want to be able to talk to their grandchildren about computers. First-time users receive help: "It doesn't take a lot really," says Angela. "It's just a confidence thing you have to build." The library is also now piloting an open-learning scheme with students from schools, colleges and small businesses, as part of a British Library project to assess what the future role of libraries could be. The idea at Ayr is to complement the work of educational bodies by helping students find things on the Internet. Around 60 people come in to work with the aid of an online tutorial and of a library research assistant, who carefully records the details of how she goes about each Internet search in a database. Angela says: "There are massive amounts of information out there but people don't have the skills to get it, and they don't know what to do when they find it. One of the roles we see for librarians is to pass on information skills to people who use the library. The teachers in the local college are just amazed at the quality of the information that is being found. They ask: 'How did you find that?' The answer is: 'I'm a librarian. I know how to look for things. I am also trained to make judgements about publishers and the quality of their material.' "

Angela says that the nuts-and-bolts material for most open learning courses still comes off packs on the library shelves, as the range of *bona fide* open-learning courses on the Internet is still limited. She foresees enormous growth in the number of self-contained learning packages on the Net, but observes that, for the present, people just need to be linked to good support material for their studies. "At the moment there is a lot of information that's free of charge, but I anticipate in the future when electronic money is properly in place there will be much more charging for these facilities. If organisations like colleges are putting stuff on the Net, they will want to recover the cost of developments. I think public libraries should build the links to where good courses are, and then it should be up to people to decide whether to give their credit card number to pursue the course."

She believes that in future, librarians will be developing their Web sites with links to sites that suit their local users and which are kite-marked with some sort of quality assurance recommendation. "The massive online library is so unstructured that a librarian's natural instinct is to make it structured for the clientele that they know, the local community. That is a natural progression from what librarians do at the moment. In recent years, the growth area has been people coming in looking for information as opposed to the book lending, which has fallen over the past 10 years. Librarians are taken for granted in how well they can guide people to information."

And what about the question of free access? At the moment surfing the Internet costs £3 an hour (£2 for the unemployed). "This is cheaper than commercial rates," says Angela. "But if a child from a housing estate comes with no pocket money, he can go on the computer and use a CD free of charge. And learning how to use a computer is free for everyone. But I think there is going to have to be a national policy on this. Legislation is in place to ensure that access to books remains free, but add-ons such as videos, CDs and Internet access have always been charged for. Funds need to be diverted into this area, because it is very important. Public libraries have remained the same for a long time, but there is now great enthusiasm for the opportunities that are here for them."

THE PEOPLE'S NETWORK

Suddenly libraries are big news. Well-respected by their customers, and used by 58 per cent of the population, they have nonetheless been in danger of being sidelined with the arrival of the information age, despite the efforts of energetic leaders like Angela McCormick. Libraries used to be the gatekeepers of free-and-easy access to information; the

Internet revolution means that a growing slice of the information pie is open to anyone, with Internet access being offered by everyone from telecommunications giants to the one-man business which sets up a couple of computers in a café corner.

Now Britain's 4,200 libraries are to be revamped to act as the focus for Britain's lifelong learners. According to *New Library: The People's Network*, a report commissioned from the Library and Information Commission by the Department of Culture, Media and Sport and published in late 1997, there are exciting times ahead. The report sets out the vision of a high-tech network that will link all libraries to the Internet, to each other and to the National Grid For Learning. They will act as one-stop shops that help people navigate all manner of information, from multimedia software for the school curriculum to databases on business training; from Web sites on researching family history to e-mail conferences with local politicians. Libraries will be a 'people's university': there is already a captive audience of 1.3 million people who visit a library every day, and for newcomers, the library is usually easy to reach and full of friendly faces. The idea is not only to encourage lifelong learning, but also to tackle the problem of information 'haves and have-nots' by giving access to computers and the Internet to people who would otherwise miss out, either because they cannot afford it or because they are too intimidated to go along to schools, colleges or hip cybercafés. As Chris Smith, the Secretary of State for Culture, Media and Sport said of the report: "Public Libraries will be a crucial part of the National Grid. Libraries, after all, are colleges for ordinary people. And ensuring access to new technology – and the wealth of information and education it can bring – through the library service means access for all, not just the few."

The estimated bill for achieving this in seven years was £750 million. "That's a bargain," says Chris Batt at Croydon Central Library, who is already doing many of the things outlined in the report. All Croydon's

13 libraries form part of Croydon Online, a community network and Web site aimed at those who live and work in the town. Members of the Central Library can search the catalogues and send requests from the comfort of their armchairs, and six schools are now linked via a high-speed network which allows them to make use of library CD-ROMs from school. The scheme grew out of a two-year project called CLIP – Croydon Libraries on the Internet, which began in 1994, a wide-ranging evaluation which led to early predictions that libraries were set to become virtual universities.

That doesn't mean that librarians necessarily become tutors, says Batt. "It could be that, as is happening here, more varied professions operate from within libraries, so the continuing education service could come and use the library as a place to educate – they do already here – and the careers service could do the same. The library becomes a kind of orchestra pit for a whole range of professions and resources. Librarians will be the mistresses (and masters) of the Universe, with valuable skills that no other agency has. But they really need to be focused – we don't want somebody to have to do a bit of everything. We need to have a variety of professions operating, together with somebody who can conduct the orchestra."

He talks about the personal virtual library – a space for customers that exists partly in the physical sense within a library and partly within cyberspace – and says that even Internet users will still want to visit the library in person: "When they want to read a novel it is far better if they come and borrow one than try and do it on the Internet. Borrowing traditional materials is still a major activity for every library – that's what they do and what people want. The development of technological resources remains at the margins, even for us, where we have quite a lot of it. But it will change when people realise that there is a growing diversity of resources to choose from. If for example, they want to search something out of a newspaper it is far better to do it on a CD-

ROM database than sit down and leaf through the newspapers. What we are also doing is making these resources available across a wide-area network to local schools and branch libraries. So we are cloning the resources wherever we want to."

He believes digital resources should be delivered free, although in Croydon charges are made to cover costs. "That was the only way we could start," says Batt. "But it is better to start, and demonstrate the worth of what we do, then find a way of paying for it remotely rather than at point of use." Batt is now involved in research into the value of the library's Web site, and in a project to look at building lifelong learning resources. His verdict: "There is lot going on – content will be everything in future!"

E-MAIL ANSWERS QUERIES

One of the most fascinating elements of the CLIP project was the way librarians used the Internet for tapping into a network of knowledgeable people, through a system called Stumpers. Built at the Dominican University in Illinois, Stumpers allows librarians to put questions which have them 'stumped' to hundreds of colleagues around the world, simply by sending a single e-mail. Questions range from the specific ("I would like to obtain a copy of a British Rail Handbook published in 1989 by Hydraulics Research Limited") to the vague ("I am trying to find the name of a song I heard as a child – I think it has 'caravan' in the title."). Usually someone somewhere offers an answer, often within the day. The reason it works so well is that librarians are disciplined users, only asking Stumpers as a last resort, and checking out answers to previously-asked questions that are kept in the Stumpers online archives to save wasting time. The Croydon librarians quickly developed a reputation for being able to answer even the most obscure questions, both for their own members and colleagues using Stumpers.

The Croydon libraries and those in South Ayrshire are members of a consortium of 130 organisations, mainly public libraries, called EARL (Electronic Access to Resources in Libraries). Founded in 1995, EARL aims to help libraries network their knowledge and resources and make them available online. Visitors to the EARL Web site can use the Ask a Librarian service to e-mail any ('factual') question to librarians, with the promise of an answer within two working days, 'if not before'. (My question on Andrew Carnegie's expenditure on libraries was answered within a couple of hours, complete with sources). There is also a wealth of pointers to online catalogues – OPACs or Online Public Access Catalogues – which have been made available by all kinds of libraries worldwide, from the world's largest, The Library of Congress in Washington (532 miles of shelves), to catalogues such as COPAC, which provides one entry point for searching some of the largest university research libraries in the UK and Ireland. Many OPACs have sophisticated search engines which, like Web search engines, accept keywords in place of exact book or report titles, so it is easy to track down the whereabouts of publications you didn't even know existed. In the case of the British Library's OPACs 97 system, users can also e-mail requests for loans or photocopies of publications in some departments, although money changes hands, not over the Internet, but on receipt of an invoice through the post.

DIGITAL LIBRARIES

One of the central ideas in *New Library: The People's Network* was to create a National Digital Library, which would widen access to the country's treasures by making digital images of artifacts and documents in museums, galleries and libraries available on line. In a number of projects around the country, institutions large and small are already digitising plum items from their collections – and seeking ways to make the effort pay.

The technology exists today – the process of digitising a historical document, for example, is basically a much more sophisticated version of scanning children's drawings into a home computer with a scanner. But at the top-end of the scale, high-quality digitisation – done with enough care and attention to detail to do justice to the world's finest manuscripts – is a slow and expensive process.

John Draper at The British Library gives an estimate of just how slow and expensive it can be: "To digitise most of the British Library, it would take 400 years and £2 billion." Admittedly, the collection is huge, and one of the world's most varied: 18 million volumes; 900,000 sound recordings; 33 million patents; 600,000 volumes of newspapers, half a million volumes of manuscripts and archives and 2 million cartographic items, plus several million stamps. "You can't digitise all that," says Draper. "You can only do it with funding for special projects or if there is a commercial demand for that material, because you need to cover your costs. Our catalogue records are digitised on a public access catalogue, so people can search for items. The next step would be to link that into delivery of electronic text or images. That can't be justified economically because a lot of our requests are one-offs. You are not looking at a rolling process of digitising books, because we don't have the money."

Draper is project manager of the Library's Digital Library programme, aimed at funding broader access to some of its material by partnerships with private sector firms aiming to exploit the growing demand for high-quality digital material. The British Library has an internationally-renowned brand name, is already used by scholars and companies around the world, and, unlike some larger libraries, its wide-ranging collections have international appeal. Four million people borrow or request copies of documents every year. Draper says: "We charge the British taxpayer a basic fee, but we can charge more for commercial and overseas services. That is the principle of how we could make money."

So far, the Library has been digitising to help preserve certain manuscripts, and to give public visitors to the galleries in London's St Pancras a chance to see more of treasured documents, which can normally be displayed only one leaf at a time. Treasures include the Lindisfarne Gospels, two versions of the Magna Carta, the Diamond Sutra – the world's first printed document, produced in China in the 8th century AD – and Gutenburg's 42-line Bible, which was Europe's first printed book. There have been beneficial spin-offs. In the Library's Leonardo da Vinci notebook, da Vinci wrote his notes in mirror-image handwriting; but the digital images of each page can be easily reversed, making the Italian text a bit less of a challenge to read. There was also a project to help scholars study Beowulf, the mediaeval poem about man against monster which is the most written-about text in the English language. In 1731 the manuscript was badly damaged in a fire, and 2,000 letters around its edges started to crumble. But in the late 18th century, before the edges fell off completely, two transcripts of the poem were made; these are now in the Royal Library in Copenhagen. In the Electronic Beowulf project, the British Library and the University of Kentucky brought together digital versions of the manuscripts and transcripts, so that ultraviolet images of the transcripts could be superimposed on to the image of the manuscript, revealing the contents of lost or damaged sections. There are also hotlinks from sections of the text to related historical material, bibliographies, glossaries and details of relevant archaeological finds. Similar techniques could be used for other documents in the future.

Draper says: "Through the private finance initiative we are hoping to be able to digitise certain works that have a commercial value – these tend to be the older, more attractive works like illuminated manuscripts which are more fragile and need preservation anyway. We are thinking of developing picture library services with a commercial partner – we would have as by-products digitised facsimiles for preservation purposes which can also be used to protect the item against being handled. But we also want to provide general access to the collections and improve our document delivery services."

Instead of having to make an expensive trip to London to see original manuscripts, scholars will in future be able to request high-resolution images to be sent over the Internet, with the aid of a catalogue published on the Web. Images in the catalogue would be low-quality, to prevent anyone using them commercially without paying copyright fees. The only problem with this arrangement, Draper says, is that it actually increases demand for personal visits to the Library. "People are so surprised by what they find on the digital image that they immediately want to check the original. Access is a very sensitive area. There is only one Beowulf, for example, and it gets handled a lot by researchers who are the top of their field, so we don't normally allow undergraduate students, say, to have access. If there is increased demand at a high academic level to see Beowulf, we can't do much about it, because it is our responsibility to provide access. But if it starts to deteriorate, that might mean saying: 'Only one person in the world can look at this thing.' That does happen with some of our manuscripts."

Some documents have lasted for more than 1,000 years; one of the issues with digitisation is that no-one is sure exactly how long electronic material lasts. Draper says: "We are still continuing to record images on microfilm, which is more stable than electronic media, as far as we can tell. Some people say electronic material can last a thousand years, through a simple process of taking backups. However, if it is on CD-ROM, the current view is that it can last 5-100 years. And if a CD-ROM was meant to be used with a particular software program, on an Apple Mac computer, for example, how do you make sure that we can read it in a hundred years' time? You have to be able to emulate software environments and that is a very expensive thing to do at the moment. The alternative would be to rip the cover off a book, scan it in as simple text and then put that into a database. That is not what we do with our books – we preserve the look of the original, the binding, the typeface, the entire thing."

With sensitivities running high over some of the collection – Newcastle, for example, is keen to have the Lindisfarne Gospels back in the North-East – the Internet provides a no-quibble way of broadening access, and re-uniting treasures now scattered around the world. Draper says: "We have Dutch manuscripts and the Dutch have English manuscripts. Some were ripped in half during the Reformation, and we have half each. You could see how the Internet could be used to bring together different collections, and allow people to compare them."

EDUCATION TITLES

The British Library already publishes CD-ROMs for schools, and plans to expand into more titles for education and the home leisure market. Karen Brookfield, head of the Library's education unit, welcomes the National Grid as a way of reaching these audiences, but believes the task is not as simple as pumping pictures over a network. "You don't just digitise materials and stick them out there – you need to do what is appropriate for the user. You need to enhance the material, add a commentary and the tools to use it. The Grid is a very convenient delivery medium, but publishing is as time consuming and expensive as delivering the content in a book or any other medium." Another issue is that although many academics work with high-speed networks and powerful computers capable of dealing with very bulky, high-quality images and sophisticated multimedia, schools are less well-endowed. "Even in our CD-ROM publishing, a lot of schools are not equipped to handle some of the things we would like to do," she says.

Although the Library already works with partners to publish CD-ROMs, Karen Brookfield says there are major issues to be tackled. "We have to sort out how so-called sister institutions treat each other, and how we treat the commercial world." Even partnerships between sister institutions can be difficult, because of everyone's need to protect their own intellectual property rights, as she discovered during the production of a recent CD-ROM on the Tudors and Stuarts. "We wanted to use images of portraits from other people's galleries. Some galleries agreed that children could use their material in the same way as they are able to use ours, printing and re-using the images within school. But others said: 'No, we won't allow that' and wouldn't negotiate, so we couldn't include their pictures – you can't have a disk with six pictures out of 600 that can't be printed."

She says the whole issue of the status of national collections needs to be explored. "If you sat in front of Magna Carta and transcribed the Latin, you wouldn't have to pay anybody a bean. No one owns the copyright in those words. But if you want to show what Magna Carta looks like, then we hold the reproduction rights of our copy. People say: 'But that's not fair, it's everybody's, it's national'. On the one hand, we agree it's not fair, but there are costs involved in housing and preserving the collections. One of the things we have not cracked yet is the use in public libraries of anything we publish."

The library is planning two CD-ROMs for adults, with two others in the series being produced by the Bibliotheque Nationale in Paris. Each will be focused on an important document, and will concentrate on a topic such as women's studies or exploration. "They will be for the interested well-educated adult," says Karen Brookfield, "But the market for them is a huge question. We sat down with the French to work out how we might sell them and it appears there is a much bigger market in France for cultural titles like that. There is a huge number of titles from the Louvre, Musée d'Orsay and the others. We do also have an eye on North America – that will perhaps make life easier. But we don't think the market is that big in Britain – we shall be very pleased if we sell a couple of thousand here."

MUSEUMS AND GALLERIES

Museums, galleries and historic sites have been quick to market themselves on the Web, where aficionados can check out everything from the Louvre in Paris to the British Lawnmower Museum in Stockport, Lancashire. They can take a virtual tour of Hadrian's Wall, Stonehenge or Colditz Castle ('Once visited, never forgotten') without leaving their armchairs – and for free. But how do institutions increase their reach, and make technology pay?

A Millennium project underway in Scotland is attempting to provide some answers. With £7.5 million funding from the Millennium Commission, the SCRAN (Scottish Cultural Resources Access Network) initiative is building Britain's only digital Millennium Monument – a huge online treasure trove of Scottish history and culture. By the year 2000, the plan is to provide everyone with easy access to 1.5 million textual records of artifacts and historic monuments, plus 100,000 multimedia items – pictures and soundclips – and 100 multimedia essays on selected topics. The SCRAN organisation is helping museums, galleries and archives around Scotland to digitise the material for their own as well as the nation's benefit.

Bruce Royan, chief executive of SCRAN, says: "We don't do the digitising ourselves – we didn't want a huge central team that spent lots of money on itself. We are grant-aiding other people to do the work according to our standards. An organisation like the Royal Commission on Ancient Historic Monuments has an in-house digitisation facility anyway, and smaller organisations tend to use bureaus. We are usually able to grant aid, which covers all the cash cost." The arrangement is that each museum retains all rights to the digital material, but grants SCRAN a non-exclusive educational licence. "That enables us to onward-licence it to any school or university without any further payment going back to the contributor. This effectively means that a primary school can just use SCRAN material without having to worry about copyright. The original rights holders can still, if they want, produce an educational product and sell it. We reckon this is quite an attractive model. It would be a tragedy if museums and libraries put on all sorts of restrictions which meant that digitised information could not be used by schools and colleges."

Multimedia essays, such as *The Scottish People 1840-1940* are being done on CD-ROM, although in future Royan says they could appear on the Web: "We are not fussed what the delivery mechanism is – we want to be flexible." The SCRAN online resource base is equipped with a search engine, and a Virtual Teacher Centre will help teachers identify how material can be linked to the schools curriculum. Work is also underway on a more graphical way of searching for material, such as being able to zero in on areas of timelines or maps. Royan says: "We think quite a lot of users will be put off by the kind of interfaces which most Web sites have got at the moment. The resource base is accessible to everybody on the Web, because we believe that education doesn't stop at the classroom door – lifelong learning or unstructured self-driven learning is part of education and we should support it. But to preserve the intellectual property rights of the contributors – because we are only taking educational rights – we only put thumbnail sketches up on the Web."

In future, he says, schools and colleges throughout Britain will be able to take out membership of SCRAN, enabling them to pull down full-blown images. Royan says: "We are actually digitising at 16 times the size of most people's screens. There is no point in doing something just for today's technology, especially if it is meant to be of use in the next millennium." After its contract with the Millennium Commission expires, SCRAN plans to continue as a self-financing operation.

⓫ The Third Age

AT the age of 70, Iris Fewkes decided that she was "getting a bit stale". In search of a new challenge, the retired garage owner from Leicester enrolled on a computing course at her local adult education centre, never having touched a computer in her life. "I wanted to stretch my mind," she says. "My granddaughters thought it was hilarious. For the first fortnight it was heavy going, but in the third week, I suddenly got the hang of it."

▲   ▲   ▲

In 1997, not only did she complete her course, but Iris was nominated as student of the year. She is now planning to use her home computer to write her life story – a bonus, as her fingers are too stiff to tackle handwriting. However, she can't begin just yet. First, her 18-year-old granddaughter Victoria has asked Iris to teach her how to use a computer. "It's a poor day when you don't learn something new," says Iris.

Not everyone is as intrepid as Iris Fewkes – this, after all, is a woman who was panel-beating and welding for a living almost half a century ago. But many people at her stage of life want to learn new tricks, and especially want to learn new technology. Why? For some, it is about keeping their minds working: 'use it don't lose it'. Others want to feel part of the modern world, in which they are surrounded – and often compromised – by technology, from the computerised catalogue in the library to the push-button timetables at the railway station. And some may realise that they, most of all, could benefit from being able to do everything from shopping to socialising over the Internet from the comfort of their own home.

Third-agers are a major force. By the year 2000, half the population of Europe will be aged over 50. People are living longer, and retiring earlier – when companies cut jobs, older employees are usually the first to go. Those who can afford it invest their savings in a PC (so much so that computer companies are now getting excited about the over-fifties sector of the market) and sign up on a course. Dr Roger Cloet of the University of the Third Age (U3A) says: "Older people have more time, and once they get hooked, you can't drag them away from computers."

U3A is full of enthusiastic learners. A worldwide organisation founded in 1972, it takes its name from the third stage of life, after childhood and child-rearing. Run on a shoestring, it is a DIY organisation in which volunteers teach local groups of people about anything that takes their fancy, often in the teacher's own home. The 70,000 members in 350 groups around Britain try their hands at everything from Latin to lipreading, astrophysics to acupuncture, with no entry qualifications required. Dr Cloet, a retired scientist, began giving courses in Bath six years ago, after he turned up at a U3A meeting to collect his wife and remarked that the set-up was "a bit light on science and technology", and was instantly volunteered to rectify the problem. Now U3A's nationwide computer expert, he travels the country giving workshops, and is currently experimenting with distance-learning techniques to train and assist a network of would-be tutors. He uses a range of outdated but still useful machines, most bought for under £20, and sees the Internet as a wonderful resource: "At U3A we have a problem – people want to have serious discussions on all sorts of topics, but they haven't got a university library around the corner. There is a great range of material on the Internet, even though the quality is a bit uneven."

Community learning networks offer great possibilities for groups like this, although some problems remain to be ironed out. When U3A had discussions in Staffordshire about using the county's new Learning Net from within schools, it transpired that after-hours visits weren't practical, as many U3A members don't like going out in the dark.

SENIORS ON THE NET

In Batley in Yorkshire, older people are being helped to use technology without having to go on courses, buy a computer, or even worry about how to switch the machine on. An enterprising group headed by schoolteacher Chris Levack – known for wiring up all the town's schools to the Internet back in 1994 – has written a computer program that allows older people to create a multimedia archive of their reminiscences. Levack says: "You place a photo on a scanner and press a button. The software scans in the photo and asks questions about it – the people, place, date, and so on. You can also add stories and comments, and put hot spots on the photo, so that a click of the mouse on the hotspot takes you to the details of the person or place in the picture. We are currently working on links to help follow one person through a whole series of photographs."

Most pictures are in black and white, and around 5000 can be crammed on to a CD-ROM, as a school resource for children working on local history projects. But the archive is also going up on the Internet, to be supplemented by archives from older people in Germany, Finland and Sweden, who will be able to search all the online material in their native languages. This follows a successful trial in Denmark, which was done, says Levack, "because we wanted to make sure it wasn't just something in the water in Batley". Levack had the idea for the project when he was trying to find materials to help children learn about their cultural heritage. He says: "I borrowed an empty shop and a colour photocopier, and invited the people of Batley to bring along their old photographs.

They would get a free photocopy in return for us having a copy. In a fortnight, I clocked up 10,800 photos. Originally I tried to get schools involved in databasing them, but they couldn't cope. As an afterthought – and I hate to admit this now – I decided that we should get the older people who brought the photos in to make the CD-ROMs."

The project, called Comma (Community and Media Archives), promises to have another spin-off. The plan is that when pictures are digitised, picture donors will hand over their copyright to Age Concern, and any profits from commercial use will be given to organisations that help the old. But Levack says the process of creating the archive is as important as the product. "People meet and have arguments – was it 1935 or 1936?; they get very little done sometimes. One photograph lasts ages."

Levack also ran a project in Batley to bring the very old and the very young together via the Internet. Seven spirited pensioners who met at the Batley Age Concern Centre on Fridays were persuaded to swap stories and reminiscences with primary schoolchildren via e-mail. Having run the gamut of basket-weaving and macrame, the group (combined age 580) was willing to try anything by way of a diversion. With the help of tutor Val Asquith, who is in her fifties ("We didn't want a young whizz-kid going to old people and saying: 'come on, log on',") the pensioners were soon racing down Memory Lane, back to the days when a Yorkshire mill-girl's wage was nine shillings a week, and there was "no messing about in the classroom". The old folks were too frail to do the typing themselves, and some could hardly see the screen, but turning them into computer gurus wasn't the point of the exercise. The vast catalogue of Batley e-mails show just how well the project helped bridge the generation gap. As one lady said: "This is teaching us to get on better with the young people. We used to think 'what we did when we were young, they don't do any more', but now we are understanding why." The Friday Group afterwards went on to write to similar groups in Norway and Denmark.

Chris Levack says: "It is important to empower older people. They should be participants in this Internet business, not just passive recipients." He envisages that, in future, the TV in the corner of every old folks' home will have access to the Internet: "When costs come down, older folks are going to spend enormous amounts of time on the Internet – especially those who are frail."

In the USA there are a growing number of networks of senior citizens using the Web. One of the best-known is Seniornet, a non-profit organisation founded in San Francisco in 1986, which encourages its 18,000 members to use the Internet to learn, socialise, and check out information on their health and rights. In the USA also, various mentoring schemes are being tried. The idea is that a senior citizen 'adopts' a schoolchild, acting almost as a surrogate grandmother or grandfather, and sets up an e-mail correspondence, giving the child an extra friend and sounding board when parental time is limited.

Companies which shed their older workforce find that a vast amount of knowledge and experience goes with it. It is often irreplaceable; in many organisations, the expert knowledge of what makes the business tick lies hidden in the depths of impenetrable computer systems, or with the people who worked in the days before computers, and who have long since left.

Chris Yapp, of ICL, says: "Lots of banks got rid of their thinkers through early retirement and they have lost wisdom – now they have lots of highly-trained people, who don't understand what a bank is for, all working longer and longer hours."

He says: "We tend to think about education as learning to think, whereas training is learning to do. We educate scientists and train technicans. Engineers in Japan and Germany are trained and educated, and have high social status. In Britain, they are neither trained nor educated and have low social status! When a bank is a bank, you tend to focus on training; when you are not sure what a bank is, how do you know what skills you need in branches when you are not sure whether you need branches? You need more people who can think. And machines can do, but people think. Are we skilling people up to do jobs that computers can do? My argument is that we need a renaissance in education in order to raise educational standards so that people can take on training as they need it. That's about their self-esteem, confidence and the ability to tackle a wider range of problems."

And that brings us back to the man we started with, 60-year-old Maurice King, in Bristol, who used technology to escape from the dole queue. If he lost his job now, what would he do? "I'd be a lot more confident," he says. "I could create my own opportunities. I'd start my own company."

INTERNET ADDRESSES

ActiVage
http://194.152.67.67/euro/activage

AgeNet
http://www.agenet.com/

Apple Classrooms of Tomorrow
http://www.research.apple.com/go/acot/

Applied Science and Engineering Laboratories
http://www.asel.udel.edu

Basic Skills Agency
http://www.basic-skills.co.uk/

British Dyslexia Association
http://www.bda-dyslexia.org.uk/#what

British Educational Communications and Technology Agency
http://www.becta.org/

British Lawnmower Museum
http://dspace.dial.pipex.com/town/square/gf86/

British Library
http://www.bl.uk/

British Library OPAC 97
http://opac97.bl.uk/

BT
http://www.bt.com

Childnet
http://www.childnet-int.org

Confederation of British Industry
http://www.cbi.org.uk

Corporate University Xchange
http://www.corpu.com

Croydon Central Library
http://www.croydon.gov.uk/frame-librarycent.htm

CyberSkills Association
http://www.cyberskills.org/

Cyberspace Seniors
http://www.azstarnet.com/~rschenk/CSS01.html

Deaf@x
http://www.webcom.com/deafax/

Dearing Report
http://www.leeds.ac.uk/educol/ncihe/

Department for Education and Employment
http://www.dfee.gov.uk/

DTI's Information Society Initiative
http://www.isi.gov.uk/

EARL Project
http://www.earl.org.uk/

EDS
http://www.eds.com

Educate Online
http://www.educate.co.uk

Education Otherwise
http://www.netlink.co.uk/users/e_o

ElderWeb
http://www.elderweb.org

Highdown Information Hub
http://vwww.com/hub/uni/highdown/

Higher Education Statistics Agency
http://www.hesa.ac.uk

Human Genome Project
http://hugo.gdb.org/

Homeschooling Information Library
http://www.home-ed-press.com/wlcm_hsinf.html

ICL
http://www.icl.co.uk/

IDC Research
http://www.idcresearch.com

Institute for Learning Technologies, Columbia University
http://www.ilt.columbia.edu

Institute of Educational Technology
http://www.iet.open.ac.uk/iet/iet.html

Interactive Services
http://www.isl.ie

JANET Information
http://www.ja.net

JASON Foundation
http://www.jason.org/

John Holt's Growing Without Schooling
http://www.holtgws.com

Journal of Information, Law and Technology
http://elj.warwick.ac.uk/jilt/

Kent TEC
http://www.kenttec.co.uk/

Kids' Space
http://www.kids-space.org

Learning for the 21st Century
http://www.lifelonglearning.co.uk/nagcell/index.htm

Library of Congress
http://lcweb.loc.gov/

Lytingale's Homeschoolers
http://www.openmindopenheart.org/EdWeb/Ed.html

Microsoft
http://www.microsoft.com

National Grid for Learning
http://www.ngfl.gov.uk/

National Homeschool Association
http://www.alumni.caltech.edu/~casner/nha/

National Literacy Association
http://ourworld.compuserve.com/homepages/nla_dlap_edu/

New Library: The People's Network
http://www.ukoln.ac.uk/services/lic/newlibrary/

Office for National Statistics
http://www.ons.gov.uk

OnLine Education
http://www.online.edu

Open University
http://www.open.ac.uk

Organisation for Economic Co-operation and Development
http://www.oecd.org

Peritas
http://www.peritas.com

Roslin Institute
http://www.ri.bbsrc.ac.uk/

Schools OnLine
http://www.ultralab.anglia.ac.uk/pages/Schools_OnLine/

Scope
http://www.scope.org.uk

Scottish Cultural Resources Access Network
http://www.scran.ac.uk

Senior Net
http://www.seniornet.org

Sister Mary of the Internet
http://www.asel.udel.edu/~stern/mary.html

South Ayrshire Libraries
http://www.south-ayrshire.gov.uk/blirc/project.htm

South Bristol Learning Network
http://www.sbln.org.uk

Stumpers
http://www.cuis.edu/~stumpers/

Superhighways Teams Across Rural Schools (STARS)
http://www.norcol.ac.uk/stars/

Thames Valley University
http://www.tvu.ac.uk

The Dalton School
http://www.dalton.org

TRENDS Project
http://www.ncet.org.uk/projects/trends/

UK Lifelong Learning
http://www.lifelonglearning.co.uk/

UK NetYear
http://www.uknetyear.org/

University for Industry
http://www.lifelonglearning.co.uk/ufi/ufi.htm

University of Paisley
http://www.paisley.ac.uk/

University of the Highlands and Islands
http://www.uhi.ac.uk

University of the Third Age
http://www.limedene.demon.co.uk/othersts.html

Vicarious Learner
http://www.hcrc.ed.ac.uk/gal/vicar

VolcanoWorld
http://volcano.und.nodak.edu/

Web for Schools
http://wfs.vub.ac.be

World Lecture Hall
http://www.utexas.edu/world/lecture/

WWW Virtual Library: Museums
http://www.icom.org/vlmp/

World Wide Web Consortium
http://www.w3.org

Xplanatory Special Needs Resources
http://www.canterbury.ac.uk/xplanatory/

WEB SEARCH ENGINES:

Alta Vista
http://altavista.digital.com

Excite
http://excite.co.uk/

Lycos
http://www.lycos.com/

BIBLIOGRAPHY

Reports, Surveys and Research Publications:

Apple Computer Inc., *Teaching, Learning and Technology – A Report on 10 Years of ACOT Research*, 1995.

Basic Skills Agency, *It Doesn't Get Any Better*, 1997.

BT, *Fax Buddies – A Mentoring Scheme for All*, October 1997.

Checkley, Kathy, The First Seven ... and the Eighth, *Educational Leadership* Vol. 55, No. 1, September 1997.

Department for Education and Employment, *Connecting the Learning Society: National Grid for Learning*, October 1997.

Department for Education and Employment, *Excellence in Schools*, July 1997.

Department for Education and Employment, *Preparing for the Information Age – Final Report on the Education Departments' Superhighways Initiative* (EDSI), December 1997.

Department for Education and Employment, *Survey of Information Technology in Schools 1996*, March 1997.

Eurolink Age, *Older People and New Technology – Report and Directory of the First European Network Meeting*, 1996.

Gatto, John Taylor, The Six-Lesson Schoolteacher, *Whole Earth Review,* Autumn 1991.

Higher Education Statistics Agency, *Student Enrolments Profile 1996/7,* May 1997.

IDC Research, *PCs in the Home,* UK Home Report Series, 1997.

Independent ICT in Schools Commission, *Information and Communications Technology in Schools: an Independent Inquiry,* ('The Stevenson Report'), March 1997.

InterForum, *Your Route to the Networked Economy,* January 1998.

JNT Association trading as United Kingdom Education and Research and Networking Association (UKERNA), *The Network Programme Report 1996-1997,* 1997.

Kelman, Alistair, Distance Learning at the LSE with Virtual Tutorials, *IT Review,* 1997(1), The Journal of Information, Law and Technology (JILT).

Kennedy, Helena, QC, *Learning Works – Widening Participation in Further Education,* Further Education Funding Council, June 1997.

Library and Information Commission, *New Library: The People's Network,* October 1997.

Marketlink Research, *Highdown Information Hub –Qualitative Research,* 1997.

McKendree J. and Mayes J.T., The Vicarious Learner: Investigating the Benefits of Observing Peer Dialogues, *Proceedings of Computer-Assisted Learning Conference* (CAL '97), Exeter, UK, 1997.

National Advisory Group for Continuing Education and Lifelong Learning, *Learning for the 21st Century*, November 1997.

National Committee of Inquiry into Higher Education, *Higher Education in the Learning Society*, ('The Dearing Report'), July 1997.

Office for National Statistics, *Labour Market Trends*, January 1998.

Organisation for Economic Co-operation and Development, *Literacy Skills for the Knowledge Society*, 1997.

Packard Bell with Michael Petre Research Partnership, *The Influence of Technology on Household UK*, October 1997.

Veenema , Shirley and Gardner, Howard, Multimedia and Multiple Intelligences, *The American Prospect* No.29, November 1996.

INDEX

FINANCIAL SERVICES IN THE DIGITAL AGE
– the future of banking, finance and insurance
by Paul Gosling

The effects of digital technology on the financial sector continue to be revolutionary. Banks, insurance companies, traders in financial securities of all kinds have all seen their business practices transformed by the advancing sophistication of digital systems undreamed of ten years ago.

In this authoritative survey the latest developments are reviewed and explained in clear, jargon-free terms and future trends predicted.   How will the digital revolution impact on insurance; on share trading; on risk assessment? An indispensable reference work for anyone working at any level in the financial services industry.

Author

Paul Gosling is a financial journalist and a regular contributor to the Your Money, Public Services Finance and Network pages of the *Independent* and the *Independent on Sunday*.

ISBN: 0 906097 54 1   Price £12.99/$19.95

RETAIL IN THE DIGITAL AGE
by Nigel Cope

The supermarket of the future may well be in your own living-room. New technology has already transformed shopping methods - both for the consumer and for the retailer - and there is plenty more to come.

This book looks at the impact digital technology is likely to have on all aspects of retailing in the light of developments currently being tried or in the pipeline. It's a book which everyone involved in retailing and who wants to stay that way will need to read!

Author
Nigel Cope is retail correspondent of the *Independent*.

ISBN: 0 906097 59 2   Price £12.99/$19.95

GOVERNMENT IN THE DIGITAL AGE
by Paul Gosling

Information and communication technology are about to achieve a radical transformation of the public sector. The management of government and the delivery of services will be completely re-shaped by the imaginative use of digital technology. Road systems, hospitals, schools and the armed services are all at the beginning of a revolution, based on new technology, which can achieve a major reduction in the cost of government, allied to much greater efficiency.

Politicians now have the technology to directly communicate with their electorate, forming a new culture of democracy, with voters stating more clearly than ever before what they expect from their representatives.

The future will be exciting, and will produce rapid change. The map to the developments which are starting to take shape is this new book.

ISBN: 0 906097 84 3   Price: £12.99/$19.95

PUBLISHING IN THE DIGITAL AGE

*How digital technology is revolutionising the worlds of books, magazines,
newspapers and printing*
by Gareth Ward

An authoritative overview of the impact of new technology on the
printed word. The book explains about on-line databases, intranets, the
different printing technologies, and on-demand printing. It surveys how
we came to be where we are today, from the arrival of desktop
publishing to the present situation where publishers are mixing and
matching the traditional with the new.

Every company is a publisher, every computer user is a publisher. Will
publishers and their customers adapt to the digital revolution or will
digital processes change the publishers? Will we need publishers – or
paper? Is it the dawning of a new era or the twilight of another one?

Author
Gareth Ward is group managing editor of the Miller Freeman Print
Group which includes *British Printer, Prepress World* and *Dotprint* – a web
site.

ISBN: 0 906097 94 0   Price: £14.99/ $29.95